UNDERSTANDING
DESIGN

KEES DORST

UNDER-STANDING DESIGN

BIS PUBLISHERS

TABLE OF CONTENTS

INTRO-
DUCTION

ABOUT THIS BOOK

Together, the 175 essays in this book provide a panoramic view over the subject of design. The essays are written to challenge designers and students of design, to reflect upon the many aspects of their field.

The idea for this book sprung from my experiences as a designer, design researcher and design educator. There is no shortage of books about design, but they tend to either be stories from practice (always nice to read, but hard to relate to your own design work) or top-heavy design theory (with no connection to design practice at all). This book tries to strike a balance, to reflect deeply and thoroughly on concrete aspects of design. It aims to be both fundamental and oriented towards practice.

In talking about 'Design', the book strives to embrace a wide variety of design disciplines, ranging from product design and graphic design to mechanical engineering, software engineering and architecture. This book deals with many issues and problems within design practice which spring from the fundamental nature of design and are, therefore, common to all design disciplines.

However, most of the examples used in the book are taken from my own discipline of product design – simply because it is always better to write about the things you know. And product design is not a bad area to take examples from. Product design problems are a combination of 'hard' technological design (engineering) and 'softer' shape design. Because it combines these different kinds of design practice, product design can serve as common ground between the various design disciplines. The examples are written in such a way that readers can easily translate these product design experiences back to their own field.

In brief, I have tried to write the book about design that I needed, but that I couldn't find in the bookshops. I hope you will find it a useful addition to the extensive literature about design.

HOW TO USE THIS BOOK

The motivation for writing this book now, is that while the education of designers becomes more and more project-focussed, there is no support for design students to help them reflect on their design experiences. The one-page essays in this book all deal with particular design experiences, and offer a student of design some foothold for understanding. To experienced designers, the essays will bring into focus many things they know implicitly. Making that knowledge explicit offers the possibility for renewed discovery and development.

Each section of this book looks at one aspect of design. All the pieces can be read independently of the others, but they are bundled together in chapters to deal with a topic more thoroughly and completely. The essays should ideally be read at the moment you have encountered a specific issue in your design work, and are open to contemplation. The peculiar format of one-page essays is meant to provide easy access to the various aspects of design. There is a general thread, though, that goes from the fundamentals and character of design to designers themselves, and on to 'external factors' like the management of design, and the role of design in society. All these issues are made very concrete by linking them directly to the experience and everyday practice of designers. The book ends with a metaphor about design.

As you read this book, you will find thoughts that range from gentle musings on design issues to passionate attacks on various misunderstandings surrounding design. There is well-meant advice, and quite a few warnings have slipped into the text as well. They are serious comments, but they should not distract from the pleasure of designing. If there is a general message in this book, it is that design is fascinating. Enjoy it!

Kees Dorst
Utrecht, 2003

THE SECOND EDITION

This is the second edition of Understanding Design. For an author, the printing of a second edition is a great opportunity to revisit the old texts and improve them with the benefit of hindsight. Over the last three years, thoughts have developed, the science of design has made some steady progress, and the world of design is going through a slow revolution. More than enough reason to start writing again.

Also, the first version of this book has sparked many reactions. The book has been avidly taken up in some places, and it has been consistently misunderstood in others. Taking all of these reactions (appreciation, as well as criticism) on board has resulted in a sizeable extension of the book. In all, 25 pieces were added, mainly in the chapters about Education and about the Future. All texts in the book have been revised for greater clarity.

I would like to thank the many students, designers and design researchers who have accompanied me in the exploration of design, and that have been a source of inspiration over these years. Especially my friends Peik Syling, Dick Rijken, René van der Veer, Frido Smulders and Rens Meijkamp, my colleagues at the universities in Sydney and Eindhoven and at the design magazine Items. The majority of the pieces in this book have been published before in the magazine of the Dutch Designers Association BNO, with the help (and patience) of the editors Hester Wolters and Sybrand Zijlstra – thank you!

Kees Dorst
Sydney/Utrecht, 2006

INSIDE DESIGN

DESIGN

AS . . .

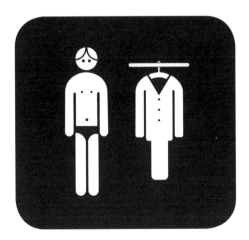

DESIGN AS APPLIED CREATIVITY

It is not easy to explain to people what it is to be a designer. They have trouble picturing what a designer does, and seem to think that you are either a vague arty-type or a hard-nosed technologist. In general your 'softer' audience will tend to assume you are a technofreak, and the technologists will think that you spend your days painting flowers on coffee machines. But what makes design so difficult to explain?

The problem is that design is not one way of thinking, but two: it is a mix of creativity and analytical reasoning. There is something peculiar about the way designers work.

This working method of designers is illustrated by a little experiment that was done by Bryan Lawson. He was interested in how designers and non-designers would tackle the same problem. So he gave a puzzle (one of those coloured block tests that psychologists like to use) to two groups of students: one group studied mathematics, and the others were designers (architects). And what happened? The mathematicians started by analysing the problem, and once they understood it, they set about solving it. All of them quickly came up with the right answer.

The designers, on the other hand, began by laying out possible solutions and tried to improve upon them. A completely different approach. Apparently, the designers were used to problems that did not lend themselves to analysis. The designers were accustomed to dealing with the chaotic problems of their profession by creating high-scoring solutions, analysing them and evaluating them. Their creativity and analytical skills were focussed on the solution, not on the problem.

This strategy can be recognised in all design professions – in many design problems, the generation of possible solutions and their gradual improvement is the only way forward. That is design.

DESIGN AS PROBLEM SOLVING

When people started trying to understand design, they of course began by comparing it to things they were familiar with. So the first model they devised was of design as a problem solving process. Cognitive psychologists had been figuring out the way people solve simple problems like 'what is my next move in a chess game': you pose the problem, search for a good solution by generating (all?) possible next moves, explore the consequences and then choose. This process of pose-search-generate-test can clearly also be recognised in design practice.

The idea that design is problem solving has led to the development of phase models of the design process, in which you first define the problem, analyse it to formulate requirements and then generate solutions. You choose between these solutions with the help of your requirements, and then implement the chosen solution (see the References section for some good books on these design models and methods). This model of design has worked tremendously well, although it has also been criticised. Like any model, it highlights some aspects of design while neglecting others. Yet, it seems that as long as the design goals are explicit, clear and stable, and a set of comparable solutions can be generated, design can be treated very much like problem solving.

If you happen to hit upon such solid ground in (parts of) your design project, you can use the sturdy problem solving model and its many accompanying methods to help you structure your design work. But not all of design is like that.

DESIGN AS LEARNING

Early hopes that by describing design as problem solving we had captured its essence were, in the end, not justified. The problem solving models of design are particularly helpful when you want to control a design process, or to make your design project run more efficiently. But the problem solving model is silent when we want to know more about design than just how to control and structure it.

This relative 'distance' from the way designers experience their work has long been a criticism by designers against the problem solving view of design. One of the early architectural design theorists, Christopher Alexander, is on record as saying that: '... <design theorists> have definitely lost the motivation for making better buildings... there is so little in what is called 'design methods' that has anything useful to say about how to design buildings... ' A damning remark, if there ever was one.

So it seems we need more models and metaphors to accurately capture design. A radically different view, which tries to arrive at a much closer description of design as it is experienced by designers, concentrates on the *learning* that takes place during design projects.

Design can indeed be seen as learning: as a designer, you gradually gather knowledge about the nature of the design problem and the best routes to take towards a design solution. You do this by trying out different ways of looking at the problem, and experimenting with various solution directions. You propose, experiment, and learn from the results, until you arrive at a satisfactory result. For instance, when you are designing, you sketch an idea and then look at it with a critical eye. This fresh look often immediately shows you what must be changed in order to improve the design. So you change it, and then you again look critically at your work, etc. Design can be described as a process of going through many of these 'learning cycles' (propose-experiment-learn, propose-experiment-learn, again and again) until you have created a solution to the design problem. In this way, you learn your way towards a design solution.

DESIGN AS EVOLUTION

Creativity in the design process is often characterised by the sudden occurrence of a significant event – the so-called 'creative leap'. Sometimes such an event occurs as a sudden insight, but often it is only in retrospect that a designer is able to identify at which point during the design process that key concept began to emerge. Such after-the-fact accounts may not be completely reliable. But we like to believe in this mythical creative leap, anyway.

When you observe designers at work you see a process that is much more gradual, like an evolution. The initial ideas can be seen as the first primitive objects, evolving and becoming more subtly tuned to the design problem over the generations. But design problems are also something like a moving target: they are usually very vague at the beginning of the design project. As the designer acquires more knowledge about the problem and about the possibilities for solving it, the design problem also evolves during the design project.

So creative design is not a matter of first fixing the problem and then performing a 'creative leap' to a solution. Creative design is more a matter of developing and evolving both the formulation of a problem and ideas for a solution, while constantly shuttling between them. The aim of the designer is to generate a matching problem-solution pair.

Design thus involves a period of exploration in which problem and solution are evolving and are very unstable, until they are (temporarily) fixed by an emergent idea which identifies a problem-solution pairing. The creative event in design is not so much a 'creative leap' from problem to solution as the building of a 'bridge' between the problem and the solution by an idea. A creative event is the moment of insight at which a problem-solution pair comes together. This can be such a triumphant feeling that it overshadows all the slow and laborious evolution that went before it.

DESIGN AS A SOCIAL PROCESS

Nowadays, designers rarely work alone. It has become almost impossible for a single designer to possess all the necessary knowledge and skills to develop a complicated design. You usually have to cooperate with other designers and consult specialists from various fields.

This means that design has become a social process, whether we like it or not. Designers need to interact with groups of people that have different ways of looking at the design problem and the design solution. These people do not only bring their knowledge to the design project, they also bring their own viewpoints, expectations and ambitions. Because they represent widely different aspects of the design, and come from completely different knowledge fields, these groups often have trouble understanding each other. Yet for the design to succeed, it has to perform well within all these different worlds (financial, technical, ergonomical, aesthetical, etc). There is no single overriding perspective that encompasses all aspects of the design problem and solution. Because of this, designing becomes a process of negotiating a consensus among all the participants who have differing interests in the design.

People who have been trained as creative designers may not be particularly suited to lead such discussions. They may be much too involved with the developing design idea to act as an independent chair in such a negotiation process. The separate discipline of design project manager has arisen to fill this need for someone who can really make the design team work together. Now that design has become a social process, designers will need to become skilled negotiators.

DESIGN AS A GAME

Design is a game with very few rules. Design problems are extremely complicated, so we must use all our wits and creativity to solve them. The results are what counts, and we will use any means to get us there.

Any design problem is a challenge, which you can master by experimenting with various views of the design problem and the many roads toward a solution. You have to choose your line of attack early on in the project, always on the basis of too little information, so it automatically becomes something of a gamble. Then you try it out, get nowhere and have to use your creativity to take on the problem in a different way. A new gamble, that may pay off – or not. And a new challenge to make it work this time.

Any self-respecting designer (and aren't we all) will also raise the stakes by adding all kinds of personal goals to the design brief. You want to make the design what you think it should be, something special. You challenge yourself by aiming high, by being as ambitious as possible. Because you have inserted your own goals, you become personally attached to the project, desperately wanting to make your ideas work. How far can you get in realising your ideal? In most of the design firms I know, the lights are on until 11 pm every night. It's a sure sign that someone in there has become attached to his ideas, and can't stop playing the game of design... It is pure fun, exciting and exhilarating. And when a good idea that you have put a lot of energy into is finally adopted, it really feels like winning. Designing is highly addictive.

INSIDE DESIGN

DESIGN
PROBLEMS

WICKED PROBLEMS

We all know that design problems are not easy. But what makes them so difficult?

Cognitive scientists, who study human problem solving behaviour, have tried to answer this by comparing design problems with relatively simple problems, like chess. A chess problem is considered to be well-structured: the chessboard is a nicely enclosed world, in which you know the value and the possible moves of all the pieces. And in chess the goal is clear: to checkmate your opponent. Despite this, solving a chess problem is difficult enough.

But compared to the complexity of design problems, chess is child's play. Design problems have been called 'wicked' problems, because none of the structure of a chess problem is present in the case of design.

To begin with, there is no fixed playing surface in design: we design in the real world, so outside influences can disturb our plans at any time. And considering a design problem from various angles will give you different pictures of what can be done to solve it – there are many perspectives, each having its own version of the truth. To complicate things further, there are always aspects of the problem that will only emerge during the solution process. So a design problem can't even be comprehensively stated before you set out to solve it...

Secondly, the moves you can make as a designer are not predefined. There are no rules in design, except the limits set by the law and your conscience...

And finally, the goals of a design project depend on the interpretation of the people involved, and they typically will shift during the design project, for instance because of what your competitors are doing. The changeable nature and subjectivity of design problems accompanies you right to the end of the project: there is not even a clear yardstick for success or failure.

FREEDOM

Design can be seen as a reasoning process, running from problem to solution. But there is no unique road that connects the design problem with the design solution – design problems can be solved in many ways. This doesn't make design irrational, though: there is logic in design, but design problems are so ambiguous that logic can be applied in many different ways. Therefore, design problems are often called 'underdetermined'.

One of the problems designers face, is that design problems are not completely fixed, but also not completely free. Most design problems seem to have a triple nature:
- They are partly *determined* by 'hard' (unalterable) needs, requirements and intentions. A designer has to reserve time in the early part of the design project to unearth these 'hard facts' by information gathering and analysis, and learn to accept these specifications.
- A major part of the design problem is *underdetermined*. The interpretation of the design problem, and the creation and selection of possible solutions can only be decided during the design process on the basis of proposals made by the designer. Thus, these proposals entail both the possible interpretations of the design problem and possible solutions to those problems.
- Part of the design problem can be considered *undetermined*, in the sense that the designer is, to a large extent, free to design according to his own taste, style and abilities. It is, of course, not the case that the designer will never have to defend these aspects of the design to others, but the designer is dominant, in the sense that he also provides the criteria on which these aspects of the design are to be judged.

In a design project, it is not always easy to see what kind of design challenge you are dealing with. How 'hard' are the requirements? How much freedom do you have, as a designer, to follow your own preferences?

PROBLEMS AND SOLUTIONS AS SIAMESE TWINS

So design problems are not fixed, but underdetermined, which means that there is room for different interpretations of what the design project should be about. This gives the designer a lot of freedom. However, it is critical that the interpretation of the design problem is relevant to the stakeholders, and that they also agree on the kinds of solutions this particular view of the design problem will lead to. The interpretation of the design problem and the possible solutions it can lead to cannot be separated. They are Siamese twins.

What then, is a 'good' design problem? To ensure a good 'fit' with the stakeholders you first need to find out what their fixed demands are. Around that core problem there is a lot of freedom, where you can choose your interpretation as long as you convince the stakeholders that the way you interpret the problem is going to be fruitful and will lead to a good solution. But you can never be quite sure about that. It helps to generate some ideas early on, as an exploration of what possibly lies ahead, but you never really know beforehand if a certain interpretation of the design problem will lead to satisfying solutions. You will only find out during the design project.

If it turns out that your interpretation of the design problem just generates a lot of dead ends, you have to go back and change your view of the problem. In practice, this is often a struggle. The design problem is the starting point of your thinking, and drastically altering your basic decisions and assumptions halfway through a design project is tough. I once observed a group of designers in which one person was clearly interpreting the design problem quite differently than the others. She saw the project as a redesigning of the current product, the others treated it as a new, conceptual design challenge. They only discovered this discrepancy quite late in the project, when they were discussing their ideas. She was overruled and had to go along in the conceptual thinking mode of the rest of the group. But she couldn't make the switch, and ended up just supporting the design process of the others without really contributing any ideas herself. She had lost her view of the design problem, the very foundation of her thinking.

BUT, IS IT ART?

In design, your goals are partly determined by others, the stakeholders, because the things you create must fulfil some practical purpose in the wider world. In art, this is not the case. An artist determines his or her own goals. They have this freedom because with their creation, artists do not aim for any practical application, but strive to influence the feeling or thinking of an audience.

Art education in the western world is focussed on the personal development of the student, so that the budding artists will be able to generate and pursue interesting goals. This goal-generating ability and their personal development, are the key issues that determine the vitality and quality of an artist. However, once an artist decides on a goal to pursue, his or her creative process looks very much like a design process. They have effectively turned their self-made challenge into a partly determined design problem. And they temporarily turn themselves into designers.

INSIDE DESIGN

DESIGN
SOLUTIONS

USER PLAN

As a designer you do not just develop a 'thing' (building, machine, product, a service...), you also propose a way of using it. This is a vital part of the new design's context. Logically the 'way of using' or 'user plan' should actually be developed first, before the design itself. The things we make do their work in close cooperation with their users, and what exactly the design has to do depends on the role we give them in this choreography. In practice, however, there are not many designers who really take user plans that seriously.

Often, designers only make some assumptions about what users do, and leave it at that. These assumptions will generally not be much different from the current usage of conventional designs, and great opportunities for innovation can be squandered in this way.

Sometimes, the development of the user plan is woven into the development of the design ('scenario building'). But more often, a rudimentary user plan is constructed only as an afterthought when the design has been finished. This explains the awful interface design of some products, and the equally awful quality of user manuals that come with most products. In design projects, manuals are almost always forgotten – they are typically made when the product is ready to be shipped to the client. Then the least busy (least bright) person of the development team will hastily be called in to make some sketches and texts, with a lawyer providing extra disclaimers, just to be safe. These cryptic texts are then professionally translated into 7 languages by people that do not know the product, and printed without ever being checked.

It is really strange that the design community, usually so professional, has this collective blind spot for the importance of user plans. Maybe designers are just so focussed on making a Nice Thing that they do not have an eye for anything else. Perhaps it is hard for designers to think in procedures. Or it could be that the development of a good user plan is a lot harder than one would think. The specialist field of interaction design has come up to advocate better treatment of the user. In a way, this should not have been necessary.

THE AESTHETICS OF INTERACTION

Design has always been a discipline that strives towards the creation of a 'thing', a 2D or 3D object. The fact that the functioning and enjoyment of that thing will only spring to life when the user interacts with it has never been much of a concern to most designers. That is, until recently. Technological advances have meant that many of the things we design are now so complex that the ability of a user to interact with them cannot be taken for granted anymore: the interaction itself has to be designed. And because such complex interactions with the design are bound to be very absorbing for the user, the design of the interaction becomes a key component of the quality that a user will experience.

This requires a completely new kind of interaction design. We need to look beyond the basic question of how to achieve the efficient and effective use of a design, and address the issue of how we can achieve quality in the interaction itself, how an interaction cannot just be functionally good but also be fulfilling. Interaction Design needs to move beyond its traditional focus on 'ergonomics-of-use', towards 'social ergonomics' and 'cultural ergonomics'. In the end, we need to develop a deep understanding of the aesthetics of interaction.

This saddles the design world with many new (and so far unanswerable) questions. The traditional design disciplines have hardly touched upon the dynamics of user interaction and have not really come to grips with the problem of designing in time (as opposed to designing in 2D or 3D space) at all. Design techniques that could be helpful in this area, like scenario-based design and storytelling, are still in their infancy and will have to be developed much further to deal with these issues effectively. As a precursor of this broader development, we can perhaps learn from the art of designing screen-based interaction in the context of computers and the internet. This new design discipline has attracted much design talent, and it has been developing quite rapidly. But even so it is still very far from mature, and many issues about the quality and aesthetics of interaction remain unresolved within this field. Everybody will recognise the frustration of trying to navigate through yet another maddeningly autistic website...

THE STORY

When you design, you are actually creating two things in parallel: the design itself and the story behind it. This story consists of all the choices you have made during your design project and the arguments that you used in making them. It is the justification of the design, which explains why the design is constructed in just the way it is.

Of course in any design project, all attention tends to focus on putting the design together. But constructing the 'story' is a vital and integral part of any design work. It helps you defend the design to others, and – perhaps more importantly – it allows you, as a designer, to keep track of the design's progression. It often happens that some of your early decisions must be adjusted or revoked in the later stages of a design project, either because they keep generating problems or because they are just unworkable. That is all part of normal design practice: you take a decision based on the knowledge you have at that moment. Later, when you have acquired more knowledge, you might live to regret those choices.

The tricky thing is to return to those early choices and revise them without wrecking the whole design. A design can be seen as a tightly knitted web of decisions which are not independent from one another. Chances are that if you change one thing, you must readjust a lot of others as well. Keeping track of the story (in notes, annotated sketches, etc) can keep you from getting tangled in your own design.

LOGIC, HISTORY AND SPYING

Both the user plan and the story behind the design might help you explain and defend your design to others. But the question still remains: How good is the design solution, really? How do you justify a design solution to a client? This is not so easy.

Explaining the logic behind the design will get you so far, and you can fall back on the design project's history to explain the choices you made. Showing the design alternatives that you considered and explaining the reason for their demise will strengthen the argument in favour of the chosen design considerably. It is worth keeping track of all your design concepts for this reason. In this way, you might convince the client that the design you made is good. But can you also assert that it is the best design, or the best possible solution? Being the best is a relative measure, so to establish a design's relative quality you must compare it to competing designs on the market. You should always be aware of these designs, and if necessary, take them apart and analyse them to the last screw. Big companies have special departments for this competition analysis, which they call 'reverse engineering'. From careful analysis you can not only learn about the rival design, but also about the ideas behind it, the technologies the competition introduced and the organisation of the production process.

But the main thing is to judge the competing product by the same criteria as your own. Providing your performance specification is well made, this will give you a good idea of the relative quality of the competition. This 'benchmarking' will give you confidence that your design will get its fair share of the market.

Of course, what you would really like to do is benchmark your new design against the new designs that the competition is developing at the same time as yourself. Industrial espionage aside, this is not possible. You never know for sure how good your design will be.

WHAT DESIGNERS MAKE

Designers make plans. They plan the behaviour of the design and its users and they plan the production of the design.

Designers' plans are expressed in all kinds of different media, depending on the design discipline. Everyone makes presentation drawings and scale drawings, but architects also make scale models, while product designers and mechanical engineers often make prototypes or computer animations. The use of these various media is a clear indication of how difficult it is to convey a design, but it is crucial that this is done well.

These plans, drawings and models are ultimately used as tools to interact with the people who are actually going to make the design. They have to take these plans and develop a way to produce the design. This turns out to be a very difficult step, which often leads to many changes to the final design. Designers, on the whole, do not enjoy this stage. Once they have delivered their plans, they see the design project as finished, and they want to move on to the next one. They do not enjoy being bothered with all kinds of nitty gritty detail problems to get their plans realised. But of course, the quality of the produced design ultimately depends on this step as well. Many delicate details can get lost when the production people find 'an easier way to make this'. So it is in the designer's interest to keep the lines of communication open and to stay involved with the design until, and even after, it is produced.

In large design projects, like the development of a car, the amount of work to be done necessitates a far-reaching division of labour. This inadvertently means that the design project is completely fractured, and that there are multiple interfaces between design and finished product. The shape designers hand over to the engineers, the engineers to the production engineers in the pilot plant, and the pilot plant ultimately turns over the design and production procedures to the production plants. When the first new model is finally introduced in the Motor Shows, the stars, the shape designers, will be giving interviews to glossy magazines while the engineers are still in 'engineering hell', ironing out final problems and getting the production up to speed.

INSIDE DESIGN

KINDS OF DESIGNING

THE DESIGNING DISCIPLINES

'Design' as such does not exist, not as a single discipline that you can clearly define or point to. This makes general discussions about 'Design' muddled from the start. What do you mean when you say 'Design'? It is even not very helpful to consider the fields of Architecture, Engineering, Graphic Design and Product Design as categories of design practice. The kinds of design work within any of these fields do not have that many traits in common, although they do display a family resemblance.

It is much more useful to choose a variety of criteria to discern different modes of designing, than to draw lines between the design professions as if they were separate species. The lines between the disciplines have always been vague and they are blurring rapidly. For instance, in all the main design disciplines, there are branches that look very much like my own profession of product design: in architecture it is the design of building systems, in mechanical engineering it is the development of small, mass-produced machines and in graphic design, the development of company logo's and house styles. Thus, it is quite common for designers to defect from their original design discipline and move to an adjacent design field.

One can think of many other criteria – besides professional categories – to use to discern types of design practice. In this chapter, we will use a number of criteria which are based on variables that do seem to directly impact the nature of design work. These variables are: the constrained nature of design problems, the structured or unstructured nature of the design knowledge needed to solve these problems, the costliness of prototyping and the amount of integration required because of the stresses of mass production. We will then look at the peculiar traditions and rituals of a design profession, and the role a designer plays during the whole process of bringing a new 'something' into the world. Both these 'softer', cultural aspects can also be extremely influential to the working reality of a designer.

CONSTRAINT

Some design problems are much more 'open' than others. They require the designer to play with concepts and ideas through a wide range of possibilities before settling on a firm direction. This takes a great deal of conceptual juggling skills. You propose ideas, look at them critically, and reconsider them. This is done repeatedly, making gradual improvements as you learn more about the problem.

Closed design problems are more like puzzles. You try out solutions, and the feedback you get from evaluating your design is immediate and clear. The assessment might even directly point the way towards a better solution. If a piece of the jigsaw puzzle doesn't fit, you know you'll have to search for something that has a slightly different shape.
Puzzle solving has its own strategies. Start where the problem is the most constrained, where there are the least choices or possibilities for error. For a jigsaw puzzle, that would be the border or the corners. Or you start with pieces that show a clear, unique image. And you always end by filling in the biggest uniformly coloured surface (the sky). However, this does not imply that this is always the fastest way, or that other solution strategies are impossible or wrong. It might also be more enjoyable to solve the puzzle in a random, browsing way.

There clearly are different skills involved in the 'idea juggling' of the open design problem and the 'puzzle solving' of the closed problem. It could possibly involve completely different types of designers. There is creativity and inventiveness involved in both, although designers often don't see it that way. It is a misconception that is kept alive by both parties. The 'creatives', who deal with more open design problems, tend to look down on the 'non-creative' closed problem solvers. And some 'closed problem' designers confirm this by downplaying the creative side of their profession. As the industrial designer Richard Stevens observed: *'A lot of engineering design is intuitive, based on subjective thinking. But an engineer is unhappy doing this. An engineer wants to test – test and measure. He's been brought up this way and he's unhappy if he can't prove something.'*

KNOWLEDGE STRUCTURE

The thinking tools available to designers depend heavily upon the knowledge structure of the disciplines that play a role in the design project. In some technical domains it is possible to reason from problem to solution in a relatively orderly way. We know a lot about the 'laws of nature', and there are some slightly more iffy 'laws of technology' that really help iron out a solution. It is even comparatively easy to translate between several technical domains (like mechanics and hydraulics) because both domains share some of the same variables.

However, this does not apply to, for instance, the fields of aesthetics and form-giving, where the knowledge base is extremely weak. It consists of some psychology, some art theory and some craftsman's knowledge of what can be done with forms, colours and textures. All of these sub-domains are completely unconnected. For every new design they have to be combined by the designer, on the basis of personal preference, taste and style. People who have tried to unite these particular subdomains on a general, non-personal level, have only come up with pseudo-theories. Several Bauhaus teachers have developed theories of form and colour which contain statements like 'squares are inherently blue'. It is easy to ridicule this, but it was an honest attempt to develop a theory of aesthetics that was every bit as solid as science or technology.

Sometimes you just wish this was possible. In conversations with clients, it is always reasonably straightforward to explain why a technical construction has to be the way it is, but it is almost impossible to convince some people of the suitability of a certain form. You suddenly have to defend your design against the clients' own personal preferences and taste. If you are really unlucky, they have already taken the drawings home and shown them to their partner who has taken a course in Home Decoration. While working in a product design firm we got around this problem by introducing the word 'formtechnical'. When asked to defend a certain detail of a design, we would say that it was 'formtechnically sound'. Just pretending to have a solid (technical) basis for a decision was enough to avoid endless discussions.

MASS PRODUCTION

The nature of a design problem is heavily influenced by the number of units of the design that has to be manufactured.

If a design has to be mass-produced, this puts an enormous emphasis on the efficiency that must be attained in the design. Integration of functions becomes vital. For mass production, you want the smallest possible number of parts (assembly is particularly expensive) made with as little material as possible, to perform a maximum number of functions. This means that it pays to use production techniques that use expensive moulds to make complex forms, as long as those complex forms really fulfil a lot of purposes. The fact that mass-produced designs are often very simple is actually a very poor indication for the complexity of the design process that led to it.

The limitations of mass production have fathered their own aesthetics. The aesthetics of doing much with little, of achieving much with the simplest possible means. Some designers can achieve great heights because of these kinds of limitations. In the last century, graphic designers of the Soviet Union and Eastern Europe developed a startlingly eloquent graphic style, making subtle compositions with large graphic elements because the printing techniques did not allow for much detail and sophistication. After the fall of the Wall, that style has gone.

The issues of absolute simplicity and integration are matters you don't have to bother with when only one item or a small series will be made. It's no use going to great lengths to integrate all kinds of functions into one part. Just design simple parts that will do the job, and get someone to put them together. Efficiency is still paramount here, but it is a different kind of efficiency: you keep the design and engineering costs low by *not* going for wholesale integration. A completely different way to design.

THE GOLDEN PROTOTYPE

Designing wisely is all about being frugal with your time. Any design problem is immensely broad, so it is impossible to list and explore all potential solutions. You have to choose and rule out options as early as possible.

Every exploration takes time, and the time commitment becomes bigger and bigger when developing concept ideas in ever more detail. You should strive to be reasonably sure about your design when it comes to the point where a prototype has to be made, because often, making a reasonably realistic prototype is as expensive as the whole design process before it. Design disciplines where prototyping is more expensive tend to build in many intermediate steps, checks and balances into their projects to avoid wasting time and resources.

That makes sense, but not for all design disciplines. If you look at web design, for instance, you would see quite a different pattern. In developing a website or an interactive system for a computer, you work on designs that are easy to replicate, and that will be used by means of the same medium on which they are made. So you have a realistic 'prototype' at almost any moment during the design process. You can do user testing at all times. Designing then changes from a linear process which leads to a prototype, into a process of continuous testing and learning. Design becomes an evolutionary process' you are able to test many generations of the design before delivery.

Evolutionary development is wonderful: the earlier you can incorporate user knowledge into the design, the better. Unfortunately, in practice it turns out that these evolutionary processes are even harder to manage than 'normal' design projects. How do you decide on the number of generations you will need, for instance? This way of working also has its own pathology, the results of which are all too familiar: the debugging drama. Software designers are often tempted to 'just make something' and then to improve that imperfect concept over many generations. But if you begin the evolutionary process at a level which is too detailed, you end up debugging a structurally bad design, ultimately creating a weak and unstable monster.

TRADITIONS AND RITUALS

One way to get a fresh look at the social aspects of design life would be to actually study designers as if they were a newly-discovered Amazonian tribe. Just as an ethnographer would hack his way through the jungle, befriend the chief, try to organise a hut in the village, and describe in detail everything that is going on around him. Most things you observe would be of a direct practical nature, just human beings reacting to circumstances in a way that is quite understandable. But some of their behaviour will be non-practical, steeped in the traditions and rituals of the tribe.

If you took this way of exploring human behaviour into a design department, you would see a lot of things that have seldom been described.
You suddenly notice that a major portion of design work consists of negotiating about information, problems and ideas with colleagues. These negotiations are often not conducted on the basis of objective information. Conclusions may be reached according to the status of one of the parties, or simple human rules like 'if you give in now on this point then I will give in next time on another'. You will also see that the people who are formally in charge of a design project are often not the ones that have the most influence. Other people in a design team might act as central 'trusted persons' and may actually be the major influence on what is decided. The network of social roles that people adopt almost never matches the formal organisation of the team or department.

A particularly telling moment in the life of such a tribe is the arrival of a new member. Initiation rites are in order. Some of the 'old' group members will take time to explain to the newcomer 'how we do things here'. This is a subtle process of indoctrination, to make sure that none of the sacred rules will be broken or traditional ways of working will be changed. Tribal identity is defined by old habits.

The funny thing is that when you confront designers with these 'unwritten rules of the game', they are immediately recognised. *'Of course, that's how it works, but you can't say so'.*

ROLES OF DESIGNERS

An important distinguishing characteristic of a design practice is the specific role the designer plays in the complete process of creation. Some architects or designers are cast in the role of the 'creative', and hand over their design concepts to technical people to iron out their construction. Others have a much more integrated approach, and actually use the technology of construction as a source of creativity.

It's hard to say which approach is better. But these organisational choices (the division of labour within a company) does have a pervading influence on the resulting design. In 'The Soul of a New Machine', Tracy Kidder describes how the project leader of a development team that is going to design a new computer, looks at the latest model of the competitor. In analysing the design, he describes it as 'bureaucratic' because two parts that could have been integrated were clearly developed separately. And the project leader decides to develop a more efficient, integrated solution by assigning both design problems to one, larger team.

Every work division creates a point of contact between people or parts of an organisation. And despite all the good ideas of how to manage these interfaces by introducing 'multidisciplinary design teams' or 'concurrent engineering', they remain a huge managerial problem. Who talks to whom about what, etc. The management sciences have been oscillating between task division and integration – especially after the shock that the Japanese dealt to Western companies with their highly successful products that grew out of more integrated development processes.

Since then we have learned that this is one of those problems that don't have one solution: both integration and task division have their pros and cons. The unsuccessful search for the one best choice has resulted in the constant reorganisation of design functions within companies, from divided to integrated and back again. Which is a bad situation all by itself. The answer to this dilemma may not lie in the organisation of the design department at all. It may lie in the commitment of the project management to create an open atmosphere where information can flow freely between all those that need to be involved.

SUCCESS

When is a design project a success? This is a deceptively simple question. In the management sciences, success is traditionally associated with speed ('time-to-market'), efficiency and Return On Investment ('shareholder value'). But some years ago, a couple of management scientists became uneasy about this definition of success. They decided to ask the people who should know, the managers, which of the development projects in their firms they judge to be successful. In these interviews they found to their surprise that there are actually two disparate kinds of projects that managers call a success, for very different reasons.

Some projects are deemed successful because they provide a great learning experience for the organisation. These are potentially really messy projects, full of friction between the parties involved ('creative abrasion', as it is called in lovely management speak), false starts, trial and error, and considerable overruns in time and cost. From a distance, one would say that this is the kind of projects that any manager would frown at. But the learning experiences were apparently deemed so valuable by the managers that for these projects, their 'normal' criteria of speed, efficiency and financial gain moved into the background. These 'learning projects' are appreciated as successes because they can be the starting point for other, less innovative projects, in which the lessons learned are 'milked' and translated into hard cash. These 'Cash Cow' projects themselves are judged purely on their speed, efficiency and financial merit.

This is an interesting observation: management scientists have traditionally selected the 'best practices' that they analyse and parade before us as shining examples of successful design on the basis of the amount of money made on a project. In doing so, they have inadvertently focussed on the second kind of project. But these routine projects cannot exist without the other, much more messy 'learning projects' where innovative design should roam freely.

INSIDE DESIGN

ELEMENTS OF DESIGN

THE RESOLUTION OF CONFLICTS

Many design problems cannot be solved within the context in which they have arisen. And if they actually cannot be solved at all, they have to be *resolved*. The way designers deal with the paradoxes and conflicts in a design situation is considered to be rather special, and a core quality of good design.

The problem is that the conflicting statements in a design situation tend to trap you in a strange thought-loop that it is really hard to get out of. For instance, the conflict could be that your design should be clearly visible and available to the user at one moment in time but should preferably *not* be visible a moment later. But physics tells us that matter doesn't just disappear. What can you do? Design something that is comparatively small, and unobtrusive? Paint it in camouflage colours, make it fold down, or inflatable? All of these are compromises, sub-optimal solutions that try to find a position within the conflict that is acceptable.

The resolution of a conflict is something radically different. It calls for a complete redefinition of the problem situation. It challenges us '...*to do what designers often do so well, namely, to satisfy potentially conflicting considerations simultaneously*'. To attain the resolution of conflicts in a design problem, the designer has to take the long way around: not attacking the problem head-on but dancing around it, playing with different ways of looking at it. If you manage to step out of the ways of thinking that gave rise to the conflict, and find a fresh and productive perspective to the design situation, then the conflict resolves itself. It just is not there anymore!

MOULDING THE DESIGN SITUATION

Imagine a group of friends getting together on a Saturday night. Let's then first give them the problem to go 'looking for a good movie in town'. And then give them a second problem, to set out and 'have a party'.

The first situation is considered to be 'problem solving', the second situation is considered to be a real design project, because there are three important differences between these two situations. The first difference is that the design situation includes the definition of the pivotal word or a possible expansion of the meaning of that concept (What *is* 'a party'? What do the different people involved *mean* by 'a party'??). There is no dominant design for what a party should be, so imagination needs to be applied at this very fundamental level. A second difference is that the design situation requires the design and use of (thought) experiments in order to get to a solution ('Shall we go to a club...?'). Thirdly, in design you have to develop tools to reach a solution, such as ways to discuss issues or arrive at decisions ('Let's vote on this, guys...').

The problem solving that involves in the 'movie choice' scenario is very simple by comparison. List the available movies, agree about the criteria ('Not too scary', 'No, I've seen that one already') and choose. Selecting can be hard enough, but it does not require a creative leap and inventiveness that it takes to mould the design situation. Design undoubtedly includes moments of problem solving, but it also contains other, more complex processes.

COMPROMISE

Any design must satisfy the many needs of everyone involved in its making and use. These needs are often contradictory, so any design project involves weighing the importance of many requirements. We aim for a design that brings the greatest happiness to the greatest number of people. This often leads to making deals and compromises. Nothing wrong with that, unless it becomes an unfortunate habit.

During my own studies, I had a tutor who helped me break that habit. I was doing a design assignment, studiously putting together a list of requirements and coming up with concept designs. Those concepts were reasonable, although I had the feeling that they weren't sparkling or innovative. Just OK. During a conversation with my tutor I expected some encouraging remarks and a pat on the back. To my surprise, the tutor really got angry, and I had to work hard to defend my ideas to him. Somehow my defence didn't work, and he brushed all my arguments aside. What was happening here? First of all, he saw my design concepts for what they were: uninspired compromises. I had tried to make a product that was OK, aesthetically, ergonomically and technically.

My tutor had seen that I had failed to make any fundamental decisions or to produce a strong basic idea in any of these areas. This became clear when I tried to justify my meagre efforts: I had been excusing a particularly awful form-detail by saying that it was ergonomically good, or technically smart. This is actually the only way you can defend bad compromises: dodge the discussion, and change the subject. The form detail was aesthetically bad and inexcusable.

This way of designing had become a firm habit with me. As a 'smart' student, I had become devilishly adept at this kind of compromise and hide-and-seek discussion. Good marks, too. And I had started to believe that this was what design was all about. Fortunately, my tutor saw right through it. He said that if I kept making compromises, I would have to defend every one of them (impossible, of course). But if I made some clear basic decisions that he could understand, he would accept almost any clear choice I made. After this traumatic event I had to start my project all over again and, of course, the later ideas also contained some compromises, but I could point out where they were, and why they were absolutely necessary. The quality of the design was much better.

WEB OF DECISIONS

If you are a designer, you will recognise the sinking feeling one gets when an idea that you are working on, improving step by step, turns into an already existing design, or into an idea you had previously rejected. You can easily get into these vicious circles because design decisions tend to be dependent on one another – a decision you take for one part of the design will affect the rest. Following where these consequences lead, you can end up uncomfortably close to where you started.

A design is made up of many of these chains of decisions, which are interconnected. Together these chains make up a very complicated network of interconnected decisions (or, not to put too fine a point on it – a giant knot). Weaving such a network takes a lot of thought, creativity and patience.

As you start a project, you have nothing but loose ends, so you begin by combining all kinds of unconnected ideas into some sort of whole. You're never quite sure whether another starting point wouldn't have given you a better, simpler web of decisions. But you have to go on connecting problems and ideas with one another. This can make designing a restless dance from subject to subject. The evolving design solution has to be cross-checked continually, because a proposal that might solve a problem in one area of the design could aggravate others.

In this process, it is really hard to keep track of what you are doing. Every designer knows the moments of complete disorientation while leafing through his piles of sketches ('What was the reason for this?'). It would be nice if you could alleviate the complexity of a design challenge by splitting up the problem into smaller parts. Unfortunately, you cannot usually do that: design problems have too many internal dependencies. Designers are experts in weaving extremely complicated webs of decisions.

INTEGRATION

One of the strongest impressions you have when you are deeply immersed in a design task, is the feeling of performing a balancing act. All of the various demands of the project's stakeholders (e.g. the producer, the user) have to be reconciled within your design. And the design must be 'good', as seen from different perspectives: it must be technically sound, ergonomical, aesthetically wonderful, and all kinds of business considerations (the production, the market, the company) must also be taken into account. Each of these stakeholders come with viewpoints, knowledge and values from their own world. In designing, you are making decisions in which all these different worlds must be combined. The process of combining different worlds is called integration.

Attaining a well-integrated design is all about getting the balance right: after concentrating on one stakeholder or perspective on the design, you must compensate for the inevitable limitations and bias of that approach by making a second step that balances the first. For instance, if a product has been designed while focusing on form, the designer will have to compensate for this bias by investigating whether the design is technically possible, producible, ergonomically sound and economically feasible. Integration-loops like these are made constantly while designing. We have already seen that you need to develop many parts of a design more or less in parallel, and with the need for integration, this means that you should develop them with all the stakeholders, and every perspective on the design, in mind. Unfortunately, it is impossible to do everything simultaneously, even for a designer. So you sometimes feel like a Chinese juggler with the absolute maximum number of plates spinning on the end of his poles. From time to time you must stop running around and create a renewed overview of your design. It is so easy to get much too involved in one pet solution, stakeholder or aspect of the design, and neglect the others.

However, there is much to be gained by striving for integration: a well-integrated design is simple, elegant and gives the feeling that 'everything has been taken into consideration, and is as it should be'. There is a glimpse of perfection in an integrated design.

COHERENCE

Integration is a hard enough goal to attain in design practice, but the problem is severely aggravated by the need to simultaneously reach coherence in your design. Coherence describes to what extent a design is 'unified', the extent to which it is free from inner contradictions, and can be perceived as a whole. The need for coherence effectively limits the amount of compromise a designer can build into a design: compromising too much will make it 'look like nothing'.

We have seen that the need for compromise and integration leads to an erratic design process of moving restlessly from subject to subject, trying to reach a balance. To attain coherence you need to adopt a clear priority and stick to it. These opposing strategies make the design goals of coherence and integration difficult to reconcile in practice. But both of them are important aims in any design project.

The resolution of a design problem can be reached by negotiating, bargaining, and making compromises. Or by doing quite the opposite: by taking a coherent standpoint and defending it, convincing all stakeholders of the legitimacy of your stand.

YEARNING FOR NOVELTY

Designers set out to innovate, to cover new ground. Nevertheless, in nine out of ten cases a new design is a creative combination of concepts that have existed before. It is already difficult to create anything novel in this sense, let alone making something that is completely new to the world. This inability to create completely novel designs can easily lead to frustration and cynicism. If cynicism reigns, design can become an uninspired cut-and-paste profession. Many of these mediocre designs will be good enough to be dubbed successful, if the market accepts them. Design then easily degenerates into being a cheap trick.

Novelty is an elusive target to aim for. Maybe it should not even be aimed for directly – if it occurs, it is often the result of a personal journey of discovery.

To avoid frustration, it is important not to burden yourself with the target of achieving Novelty in every project. But you should strive to always do things that are new to you, irrespective of the novelty-value they might have for the rest of the world. In doing things that are new to you, it is quite possible that you will sometimes 'reinvent the wheel'. This may even be necessary – only if you come up with an idea yourself will you really understand it, get a handle on it and realise what you can do with it. The longer and more intense your journey of discovery, the further you will be able to wander off the beaten track, and the greater the chance that you will eventually achieve Novelty in your designs.

Whether you actually achieve Novelty then ultimately also depends on many other things: the design challenges you get, the people you work with – and on something called pure luck.

WHEN ALL ELSE FAILS

Design problems can be acutely paradoxical. The different stakeholders (producers, buyers, users, society) of a design project often have contradictory needs. This can make life very difficult for designers, saddled with the task of creating something which will somehow satisfy all these parties.

And as a designer you do not have the luxury of choosing one side of the paradox over the other – you have to create a solution in such a way that the paradox is resolved. This is actually what stakeholders expect from designers, to be magicians that conjure a simple design that satisfies everyone!

Surprisingly, this is often possible.

But sometimes a paradox is so fundamental that it just cannot be resolved, no matter how hard you try. Returning to the brief, you have to negotiate with the parties involved, explain your predicament and convince them to lower their ambitions a bit. This, of course, is not what they want to hear and it involves a good deal of persuasion. You have to convince them on the basis of an extensive analysis of the possibilities that they really have to lower their aims to arrive at any solution at all. But it remains a tricky situation. In most stories, the messenger isn't the one that lives happily ever after.

WHY DESIGNERS DON'T DOCUMENT THEIR PROJECTS

A design problem is a situation of tension, of unattained aims and unresolved conflict. This tension is the force that initiates and drives design.
At the end of a design project this tension is more or less relieved.
Once a design problem is resolved, it disappears from the mind of the
designer. This is very much like any form of problem solving. The philosopher Ludwig Wittgenstein has stated that: '... *we are aiming at ...*
complete clarity. But this simply means that the philosophical problems should
completely disappear. The real discovery is the one that makes me capable of
stopping philosophy when I want to.'

Design, however, does not take place in the pure and abstract world of
philosophical thought. The world in which we design is much too complicated, contradictory and changeable to allow for such a complete
resolution. There is always room for improvement, and although design
projects end, a design itself is not stable – it will change over time.

These changes are much harder to make when there is no record of why
the design was put together in the way that it was. The later 'improvements' might disturb the design, and effectively destroy its coherence.
Because of the difficulty of making changes, there is always pressure on
designers (from their employers) to document their work in great detail.
Designers tend to resist this – during the project they want to continue
designing, and anything remotely like bookkeeping is often against their
nature. After the design project, the documentation task becomes very
difficult – designs are tangled webs of decisions which are so closely
dependent on one another that is impossible to find a logical point to
begin the explanation of the how and why. And the resolution of a design
problem makes it hard to imagine that certain things were problematic
at one time.

INSIDE DESIGN

HOW TO

....?

IN PRAISE OF COMMON SENSE

Designers are convinced that 'design' is a special way of thinking, and they spend a lot of time trying to convince the rest of the world of this. They are using this argument to battle against a lack of recognition. Well, they could be wrong.

What always surprises me is that seventeen or eighteen year old kids, new to design school, seem to have very little trouble doing design. At a simple, basic level of course, but they manage. It doesn't seem like they first have to learn an alien, fundamentally different thought process. Apparently there is a certain level of design that can be approached by common sense. Sounds disappointing – we would rather be something special, but there it is. But what is common sense, anyway? It is a deceptively unassuming name for an extremely complicated set of thinking strategies that we use to navigate through the world. The things you never explicitly learn, but that you absorb as you grow up. Only the most avid Artificial Intelligence enthusiast would claim that we are ever going to get common sense into a computer.

Apparently, the difficulty in design is not reaching that first level of seeming competence, it is attaining the higher levels. An experiment has shown this quite dramatically. Researchers gave the same design assignment to second year product design students and to designers who had just graduated. As it turned out, the second year students saw the assignment as a simple problem, and sketched away merrily. This was in stark contrast to the graduates, who entangled themselves in enormous amounts of information, making long lists of requirements. Apparently, they saw the problem as being much more complicated. The design school had been very successful in teaching them the complexities of design. Unfortunately, it turned out that they still lacked the skills to also solve a complex problem in the few hours available. After much groaning and frowning, they came up with rather boring solutions. When the results were graded by experienced designers, the second year students got the higher marks. Apparently it is possible to unlearn your common sense design ability.

INFORMATION

It is important to get a fair overview of the information that could be relevant to the design task early on in the design project. But don't overdo it. As the architect Richard MacCormac observed: *'I don't think you can design anything just by absorbing information and then hoping to synthesise it into a solution. What you need to know about the problem only becomes apparent as you're trying to solve it.'*

Some designers become quite 'information happy' at the start of a design project and spend a lot of time collecting it. This is suspicious behaviour. It can be a way to hide from the problem, a subterfuge for not wanting to confront the creative step of the design project. Or, even worse, it could be masking indecision. Some people like to collect loads of information in the hopes that the information will somehow settle some difficult issues for them. It never does.

And in design, information is precious: gathering it takes a lot of valuable time. Information collection (after the initial broad exploration) has to be limited to the things you think you can use. Specialists, or other 'significant others', are an important source because they have the knowledge and can place it into a context, so they pre-select the information for you. A designer has to be able to talk to an enormous array of specialists. Generating enthusiasm to plunder their brains is a key design skill.

The internet, on the other hand, is an information gathering disaster. Whenever I give a design assignment to my students, they immediately go to The Medium, and start cutting and pasting loose bits of stuff. As a teacher, what you then get is a nice pile of incoherent reports that are all based on the first ten hits from Google (so much for the unlimited information on the World Wide Web). You cannot blame students for trying to get their information in the easiest way possible. But knowledge that is selected without a proper understanding of context is just unsorted, uninterpreted and unreliable data. It does more harm than good.

GENERAL TO CONCRETE

The consensus among designers is that the best practice is to slowly work your way from the very general level of an assignment to the concrete level of the end design. This is the opposite of jumping to conclusions – it is more like crawling to conclusions. There are two reasons for this.

Immediately going into the details of your first design idea limits your view enormously. If you fail to explore the design problem, with all its hidden traps and possibilities, you will have no idea whether the design you are working on is good. 'Quality' in design is not an absolute measure, it depends on what other designs are possible. You need to have a general overview of what is possible in order to defend your design. And there are always competitors who haunt the same design area... You need a thorough exploration to prevent surprises.

Secondly, there is a question of efficiency. Detail design work is laborious. You cannot afford the risk that the detail you have slaved over will not be needed, or will have to be altered beyond recognition.

This means that designers spend part of their project in an artificial state of ignorance. They could have gone into detail a long time ago, but they don't. They talk in vague terms about the design, and make sketches that could have been much more definite. Designers know that they must first figure out the more general levels of the design. In fact, this is one of the problems with most computer sketching programmes: the pictorial quality is too high, everything looks much too realistic to support an explorative sketching and thinking phase. You really need vagueness, not a nice presentation drawing.

Naive design is always quick. Contrary to what you might expect, good design schools teach you to slow down.

SEVERAL OPTIONS

Designers and design theorists agree that it is important to always develop several design options in parallel. Which, at first sight, seems like a waste of time and effort. Wouldn't it be more efficient to take one good design idea, and develop that as quickly as possible?

The importance of developing several options in parallel lies in the role these design concepts play in exploring the problem. In the beginning of a design project you have to try out different directions before you can find a promising route towards a solution. The different directions will tell you what the design problem is made of and will give you an idea what difficulties or limitations might be encountered later on. Only trying one road is simply uninformative, an insufficient exploration.

Having several options can also help to explore what the client really wants. The client's vague ambitions and needs contained in the project brief, are never clear enough to guide you to a solution. Confronting the client with several concrete design proposals can elicit much more informative reactions – the kinds of reactions you certainly don't want to hear at the presentation of the final design, when it is too late.

You also need several design options because design quality is a relative thing: you can use the other concepts as a benchmark for the final design. You use them to justify your choices in the final design and explain its merits to the client.

Still, the development of design options is something that should be done economically. You cannot just triple or quadruple the design effort for nothing. To work well for all these various purposes, design options should not just be variations on a single idea. They should be based upon different interpretations of the design problem, or based upon clearly stated priorities. If these priorities are chosen well (and preferably on the extreme side), the following mini design processes will definitely lead to radically different results. Only radically different designs will help explore the design problem and its possible solutions.

MEANS AND ENDS

It is really important in a messy process like design, not to confuse the means and the ends. That is why most methods for controlling the design process start with the formulation of something like a 'problem statement'. This contains the aims of the project, in very concrete terms. A problem statement is often difficult to formulate, but it pays to spend some time on this, because you can only work efficiently if you know what your goals are.

If you don't have a problem statement, or if it is too vague, you will encounter conflicting opinions about what the problem is later on in the project. This typically happens at the conceptual design stage, when design ideas have to be evaluated and selected. If the designers within the team have all been solving a different problem, they will never agree on what the best solution is – their criteria for what the design should be are widely apart. The ends do not match, so the design proposals (which are a means to attain these ends) won't match either.

It will be impossible to choose the 'best' solution. You then get into a discussion where every designer will defend his own pet idea, and by implication their view of the design problem. After all the work they put into it, they will probably not be very open to the suggestion that their idea is a great solution, but for the wrong problem. This can lead to unpleasant fights among otherwise very nice people.

CONCENTRIC DEVELOPMENT

Design projects can easily become skewed. We often tend to become a bit too enthusiastic about a certain part or aspect of our design problem. If we let ourselves be carried away the interesting features get all our attention. Other aspects, that may be just as vital to the functioning of the final design, can be undervalued or even forgotten.

I once observed an experienced designer getting completely carried away with one aspect of his design, championing the cause of the users to such a degree that he actually aggravated technical problems in the construction to the extent that they were no longer solvable. He only discovered this when it was too late, and he had to abandon the design problem.

The solution to this is called 'concentric development', which recommends that you develop all aspects of the design to the same level of detail before you decide to go on to the next phase. It is as if you keep circling around your design, looking at it from all sides. In doing so, you make sure your design stays balanced – not necessarily at every moment in time, but at least at the moment you make important decisions.

OVERVIEWS

Keeping an overview of your project is quite a problem in design. It takes valuable time to regularly step back and assess the mess. It is not so easy either: as a designer, you are often completely engulfed in your project, struggling with the design problem and juggling possible solutions. It is difficult to muster the necessary distance and appraise your efforts with a cool eye.

But there are natural moments to do this. Since you always work on a design project in sessions, which vary in length from a few hours to a complete day, it would be good to create a brief overview of the design project at the end of each session. This overview can serve to keep the project on track, and also act as a starting point for next session.

Still, it is easy to get entangled in your web of information, design decisions, ideas, etc. Experienced designers tend to work, if not systematically, at least in an ordered way. They make piles of different kinds of information, and make notes of the most important conclusions. They use their office and their desktop as an 'external short term memory'. Design offices are always fun to see. Designers more or less live within their projects.

DECISIONS

It helps to remember that, as a designer, you do little else but prepare decisions for the client to make. You provide the basic material, in the form of problem statements, lists of requirements, design ideas, test reports, etc, so that the client can steer the course of the project.

Thinking about design in this way does help to solve some eternal issues of design projects. For instance, the question: 'How detailed should a design concept be?'. Answer: 'Detailed enough for the client to decide in which direction the project should go'. This involves having a good overview of the basic design idea, a comprehensive view of what the design is going to be like, and a reasonable certainty that the design concept will not get into (technical) difficulties later on in the project. So there is some detail design work involved on suspected critical points, but not on others.

The designer, in preparing the ground for these decisions, has the opportunity to influence them considerably. You know which concept you want to be chosen, and it is tempting to subtly 'rig the vote' by presenting it in a better light than the others, perhaps by elaborating on it more during the presentation, or by putting a little bit of extra quality in the drawings.

That is a strange behaviour. You pretend 'objectivity' regarding the work you developed yourself, but that is quite unnecessary. Apart from being a designer, you should also take on the role of a design specialist who advises the client on which direction to take.

CYCLES WITHIN CYCLES

The natural way to tackle any problem, including a design problem, has been described in a little model called the problem solving cycle. The model states that you should first analyse a problem, then create a solution (this is called synthesis). The next step is to simulate the behaviour of the solution to see what it does, and then evaluate the solution. This is a cycle, because after the evaluation, you can decide to go through the process again if you are not completely satisfied, or start a new cycle to tackle a different problem.

This is just natural behaviour: it is how you solve all practical problems in daily life. Design is no exception. A design project can be seen as an accumulation of hundreds or thousands of these miniscule problem solving processes.

In a design project these problem solving processes are nested: you have small, local cycles that take a couple of seconds, and bigger ones that take days or months, which consist of many smaller cycles. Each design phase is a cycle of its own.

This even holds true for the complete design project, which can also be seen as one huge cycle of analysis-synthesis-simulation-evaluation. In this mega process, analysis includes orientation on the problem, seeking relevant information through research and making a problem statement and programme of requirements. Synthesis includes several rounds of idea generation and analysis. Simulation includes making drawings and possibly the production of a prototype. The evaluation of the final design and the project as a whole can plant the seed for the next project.

THE LIMITS OF PLANNING

It is difficult to plan a design project. You never know how hard it will be to gather the necessary information, or how much time it will take for good ideas to surface, and you never know how often you will have to 'iterate': to go back to an earlier stage of the design project because you have reached a dead end. It is impossible to predict and plan design. Notwithstanding all these uncertainties, you still need a plan, otherwise the whole design process spins out of control.

In planning design, you need to ascertain at which moments decisions must be made. Design decisions are based on information that is never going to be complete – and there is always a tendency to keep gathering information and postpone decisions. The same is true for the development of design concepts – they are never going to be complete to the finest detail before you have to choose between them. Planning can help force the necessary issues at the right time, so that the whole process will keep moving forward.

A design plan must be dynamic. As the uncertainties about the course of the project gradually diminish, you constantly need to adjust the planning accordingly. Most designers do this by working with a general plan that is more or less static, setting the major deadlines for the delivery of (intermediate) results. This is the basis for the detailed planning that only covers the week, or weeks, ahead. This short term planning is important because it specifies the workload of the designer, and protects a designer against unrealistic expectations and pushy project leaders or account managers who have promised too much to the client (the very dynamic *'Oh yes we will do it right away'* types).

If the design project runs into grave difficulties, the general planning will have to be adjusted in consultation with the client. The short term planning has to be kept realistic at all times: nothing is more demoralising than an impossible planning.

RULES OF THUMB

Each design profession has its own rules of thumb, the vague but proven knowledge that will almost inadvertently drive many design decisions. These weak 'rules' are really hardly worth the name. They are often very obscure, and it is usually completely unclear when they should be applied.

An example. In product design, you are advised to always try to use rotations, and not translations, to make something move. Rotation around an axis (as in a hinge) is cheap and can be made with all kinds of bearings that are very dependable. Sliding something along a rail is asking for trouble. Slides always get dirty, break down, and are much more expensive to make and maintain. This is both true and false. The utility of the 'rule' depends very much on the concrete design situation. This is applied wisdom at a pretty detailed level. Knowing what to do and how to make things. You have rules of thumb for just about every aspect of design practice – things as diverse as the art of making a good marketing questionnaire to the firm advice not to use circles in a graphic composition (they draw too much attention, somehow).

Design is particularly hard to capture in a model or theory, it seems to defy the imposition of rules. But it is rich in these 'rules of thumb', and they play an important role in many design decisions. If you ask designers 'why?' you could easily collect them. A study was done into the rules that guide the behaviour of design project managers. After following some 40 projects for twelve weeks about 450 rules were formulated, ranging from the very simple and obvious to very sophisticated, and it was clear that these weren't all.

There was a time when a lot of research was done into our rules of thumb because they were seen as the building blocks for expert systems, computer systems that would be able to hold and apply knowledge, much like a human expert. The sheer complexity of the rules, their vagueness and the impossibility to pinpoint when they could or should be applied, has more or less defeated this ambition. Still, it is useful for us humans to think about the rules of thumb, and notice when we use them. That will make it easier for us to break them when necessary.

PRIMARY GENERATORS

There is an endless discussion in design research about where the first idea comes from. But somehow, the first idea is always already present.

You always have something in mind when you start designing, some initial image that was evoked by the words of the assignment. You cannot think about a design assignment without this first inkling of a solution. These first ideas are called 'primary generators', because they are the starting point for many subsequent design ideas.

It is important to get these ideas, as well as vague inklings of solution directions, out into the open immediately. Start writing them down or drawing them right away. These first ideas can be full of assumptions that are too vague to pinpoint, and therefore hard to question or reject. If they remain implicit, they might hamper the design project by limiting the range of solutions to be considered.

And they can be incredibly persistent. The architect Rowe has observed that: *'A dominant influence is exerted by initial design ideas on subsequent problem-solving directions... Even when severe problems are encountered, a considerable effort is made to make the initial idea work, rather than to stand back and adopt a fresh point of departure.'*

In some brainstorming techniques this problem is recognised, so you begin with a round of 'purging' where you just name the initial ideas and put them aside. The next rounds of brainstorming are then aimed at surpassing them in every respect.

BADLY MUDDLED

In almost every design project that I have worked on there have been moments of total confusion. A feeling that your creativity is getting you nowhere, and that any next step you can think of will probably be counterproductive. This feeling is particularly strong when you get into design's little vicious circles.

It can happen that a train of thought which began as an original and promising new view of the design solution ends up being incredibly close to an idea you had before. Not a very satisfying feeling.

Another vicious circle always happens when the problem statement, which is the starting point of your design project, just doesn't differ enough from the problem statement that gave rise to the current design. You can do as much research as you want, and generate ideas forever, but as soon as you start detailing your 'new' design concepts, the requirements will make them gravitate slowly but inevitably towards the current design. The end result of the whole process is that you rediscover what was good about the original.

If the problem statement contains no real reason for change, the whole design effort will come to naught.

DESIGNING A CONTEXT

In the ideal design project the client is eager and involved, the designer can really use his creative potential, and their collaboration leads to great ideas. All decisions are made smoothly, in an inspired atmosphere. Design can be wonderful. Those dream projects only occur ever so often. The context of most projects is that the client is pretty uncertain in his ambitions, and is afraid that an extreme or novel design won't do well on the market. In most projects the designer has to fight for every scrap of freedom.

Why are some projects so enjoyable, and others not? How can you create a dream project?

When a design project takes place in the context of an original initial vision, which is shared by both the designer and the client, it will lead to an original and strong design. Normally, the existing design acts as the implicit context for the new design. This implicitly fosters a resistance to change. When you think about it, you really have to design an original vision of the future to serve as the context for the new design before you can start the design project itself. To create something really innovative, you first have to get rid of old ideas and build a new frame of reference. This actually happens quite naturally in most design processes: you gradually change the client's frame of reference, through the development of design concepts. Unfortunately, since the most vital design decisions are made early in the project when the old frame of reference was still dominant, this process usually doesn't go far towards a new outlook on the problem. By the end of the project you often feel that there is finally some room for manoeuvre, but then it is too late...

So, you should begin a new project by explicitly making a new frame of reference, by looking critically at the assumptions and preconceptions that underlie the current product, and also the 'new' design assignment. Once you question these assumptions and replace them by a new vision, you are free to design something radically fresh and innovative. The new design will then be judged against the new frame of reference, instead of against the old, and it will fit naturally into its context, no matter how revolutionary it is.

HINDSIGHT

It is often hard to learn from your design projects, because they are all so very different. Knowledge you have picked up in one project can't often be applied in the next one. This is true for design education, as well as for design practice.

At Stanford University they have got around this problem by experimenting with a new design curriculum layout. The students receive a really complicated design assignment, and have to come up with a design and a model of it in just a couple of days. When they have finished, they get the same assignment again, but now with two weeks to complete it. Finally they get it for a third time, with the six months that you realistically need to develop the product.

What happens? Well, in a few days you can always make something, but it isn't going to be very good – it will only be a sketchy embodiment of your first idea. In two weeks you are able to generate more ideas, and do some research. You cover some ground, but you'll mainly discover how much more needs to be done to really achieve a good design. So, it comes as a relief to get the six months you need to do the job properly. The students now benefit from all the things they had learned about the problem and solution in the first two run throughs of the project.

This method of working out a project several times has also been adopted by design agencies. It is wonderful way to embark on the exploration and learning that is part of any design project. And forcing yourself to create a complete result (model) in every run gives very good feedback on the possibilities and difficulties of various lines of attack. Design firms also often try to get the client involved in these 'pressure cooker' sessions, so that the client learns what to expect in a design process, and the foundation of a good cooperation with the client's people can be laid before the real project begins.

In design, it is always a pity that you only understand what you should have done at the very end of the project. This method is a way to generate that knowledge early on, so that you can begin your project with the benefit of hindsight.

HOW NOT TO DESIGN

Hard as it is to say how to design, it is easy to say how *not* to design. Apparently, what constitutes a successful way of working depends very much on the specific design problem, the situation and the character of the designer, but failure and incompetence are universal.

OK, how do you fail as a designer? Well...

- Always cling to your first idea.
- Jump into the details immediately.
- Solve one aspect of the problem first.
- Ignore a stakeholder, preferably a vital one.
- First design the form, then sort out how the thing should work.
- Promise too much to the client, really inflate his expectations.
- Don't listen to your client, lie to him if necessary.
- Be inflexible in your ideas and approach.
- Try to surprise your client with a completed design.
- Ignore any tests that say the design might be below par.
- Wait for inspiration.
- Stay 'fresh' by not gathering information.
- Do not plan (because that takes too much time).

And so on.

This is a good but uncomfortable exercise in self-reflection. We are all sinners, some of the time.

ABOUT DESIGN

THINKING ABOUT DESIGN

THINKING ABOUT DESIGN

People who have thought about design have done so in many different ways, motivated by a variety of reasons. To managers, design is important because there is a lot of money involved in design and innovation projects, and so they have developed methods to control design processes. Sociologists have described design historically, as a crucial component in the making of our brave new technological world. Psychologists have tried to model the creativity that plays such an important role in design. All of these standpoints, and many others, touch upon widely different aspects of design.

Most importantly for this book, designers themselves have become interested in understanding design, to improve their own performance. But how can you ever gather enough knowledge to thoroughly reflect on an elusive, complex and creative process like design?

The good news is that most of what we would like to know about design exists already, hidden deep inside the brains of designers. Good designers know how to tackle design problems in very successful ways. The bad news is that they are not usually able to explain to others what they do, why they do it, and how. The complicated and creative nature of design means that most design knowledge is implicit – and is notoriously hard to bring out into the open. Design researchers therefore observe designers at work, interview them, and try to make theoretical models that they hope will capture the essence of designing. This is the scientific way to gather objective knowledge about design in order to pass it on to design students and professionals.

After early hopes to the contrary, design researchers have realised that they can never capture all of design, nor completely understand or model it.

REALISM VERSUS CLARITY

Thinking about design can be somewhat paradoxical. On the one hand it is fascinating to try to understand what happens within a design activity. But on the other hand, when you read what design researchers have to say, it feels like design practice with all the fun left out. Dry, abstract descriptions of a very exciting occupation. This is not easy to avoid, because some amount of abstraction is inevitable: you have to step back and take a detached look if you want to describe something. If you would stick closely to the reality of design practice, and manage to describe design in *all* its complexity, you would end up being swamped in detail. You would be unable to get any kind of overview at all, let alone develop helpful advice for designers. So any general statement (theory, model or method) about design must sacrifice some realism for the sake of clarity.

Case studies and anecdotes from practice can feel much more 'real' and appealing, and in their richness they can be of great help to designers. In such accounts design is described holistically, nothing is left out: process, people, design problem and the context of the project are all included. This makes a well written case study a pleasure to read, much livelier than any abstract theory on design will ever be. However, the drawback of case studies is that it is difficult to pinpoint what you should learn from them. People can interpret such 'rich' stories in any way they want, and they can always be interpreted to confirm your preconceptions.

I have approached this dilemma by dividing design into small subjects, and looking at design from many different angles. These facets of design can be described in one page which is meant to be clear, concrete and succinct. All these pieces together then form a general but detailed picture of design, much like an image is built up out of many coloured pixels.

DESIGN SCIENCE:
THE PLEASURE OF ABSTRACTION

Since the real world is much too chaotic for us humans to understand clearly, we use a trick called abstraction. In considering something in an abstract way, you try to ignore all unnecessary details. Abstracting is a process of putting things between brackets.

Design researchers who have developed models of designing have done so by focussing on the dynamics of design processes, and they 'bracketed' everything else. They completely ignored the properties of the designer, the design problem and the design situation. The various phase models of design are examples of this limited way of thinking. It is claimed that these models are purely process-oriented, and that they could therefore be applied by *all* designers to *all* design problems in *all* design situations. These sweeping claims are part of the pleasure of abstraction.

These abstract models of design take many steps back from a direct design experience to reveal patterns in design processes. They are extremely useful for managers because the patterns enable us to 'objectively' control design projects much better than before. But they are so abstract, so far removed from what designers experience, it is like they are looking at design from the outside. They are never going to help us inside a design project, working through our problems and solutions. They are about controlling design processes, not about doing design.

DESIGN PRACTICE:
THE PROBLEM OF APPLICATION

Can you talk about design in an exclusively process-focussed way and still make sense? You ignore so much that is interesting, and also difficult, about designing. The art of design is all about the intricacies of choosing the best actions to take in a concrete design situation, which very much depends on the specific design problem you are dealing with and your own abilities. The art of design is linked to the designer, the design problem and the design situation, not just to the process of designing.

The big trouble with abstraction is that people tend not to go further. Once they have bypassed the messy details of everyday life by developing a wonderful theory or method that works within the abstracted world they constructed, they leave it at that. They present the method to the world as a new piece of truth, write a book about it and start a lecturing tour.
But this is where the real problems start for practitioners. By abstracting, theorists put many aspects of reality between brackets. When applying such a method in real life, those aspects that they conveniently left out come back to haunt us (us, not them!).

Sadly, design research is no exception to this. Most design methods that have been developed over the years are basically correct in what they say. But they are very hard to apply successfully. What we miss is a manual with instructions for use, linking the method to our own concrete design situations. When should I apply a certain method? When is it not appropriate? How should it be applied? Often it is not even clear what the consequences are of using it.

This is why most design curriculums are built around a lot of design project work. Let students live their own case studies, and have an experienced designer come in to help make sense of them.

SCREENWRITING

Theoretically, it should be possible to establish detailed methods for design practice, if only we would be able to combine our knowledge about the design process, the design problem and the designer into a coherent whole.

I never thought this was realistic, though, until I read the Screenwriter's Workbook. In this amazing little book Syd Field presents the rules of practice for writing a (Hollywood) film script. Based on a detailed view of the dramatic structure of a movie, a keen knowledge of the writing process of a scriptwriter, and his feeling for the motivations and troubles of an aspiring writer, he delivers a very detailed description of the writing process. The method that he constructs using this description is unabashedly prescriptive and almost aggressive in its assertiveness: after your initial idea has been developed, you should write a four page summary. *'Not two pages, not ten pages, but four'*. And he gives valid reasons for all his golden rules. He knows how many acts and scenes it takes to tell a story, and that the main dramatic development, in the middle of the movie, will take place on page 60 of your manuscript.

Of course, this all sounds like a much too restrictive framework for a writer to work in. You suspect that his method could only lead to very banal, standard movies. But the examples Syd Field gives are very diverse, and include some movies you really liked and experienced as being original. It is not easy to dismiss his method, because apparently he really does know how these movies work.

There is no fundamental reason to assume that something like the Screenwriter's Workbook would not be possible for other design fields. But do we want such absolute methods?

THE EXPERIENCE OF DESIGNING

DESIGN EXPERIENCES

The basis for the insights of this book is provided by the experiences of designers and by design research. This focus on experience may sound a bit soft. What, after all, can you say about experiences? They are so personal and subjective.

But we are all designers, so we all face the same problems that are associated with design, and we are all influenced by the context in which we design. We are probably also a bit alike, at least we are fascinated by the same kinds of challenges. This means that we should be able to talk about shared experiences, and that we can do this more or less objectively.

Experiences are not necessarily vague. They are what we notice and feel, and this is very real, very concrete (in fact, much more concrete than the theories and models of design research). I do not aim to generalise the design experience, or to explain it in a psychological way, but just to describe design experiences, and to link them to the character of design and to the context in which we do design. Those connections can be made quite clearly, too. It is for the reader to connect the experiences and reflections in this book to his own design practice.

INSIDE DESIGN

Design can be captivating. If all goes well, the design problem is interesting, your ideas flow nicely, and you are in another world. Nothing exists except your own thoughts, decisions, sketches, doubts. The work seems to hardly take any energy, and to have its own dynamics. This feeling of 'flow' is really addictive. Getting your teeth into a design problem and coming up with good ideas can be a real kick. And there is real sorrow in having to take leave of an idea that looked promising but turned out to be less than satisfactory.

Design is such a diverse profession that it becomes very much like life. You use everything you have to solve a design problem: all your knowledge and personal experiences, your creativity, and your powers of thought. It engulfs you completely. You become sensitised to the kinds of things you are designing, whether it be buildings, constructions, products or graphics. Being a designer changes the way you look at the world. Design is more than a profession, it is a way of life.

This is what design looks like from the inside. From the outside, design is a strange profession – the creation of novel things by means of an incredibly messy process that is hard to control and difficult to rely on.
The marked contrast between the inside and the outside point of view causes no end of misunderstandings between designers and the outside world.

LAYING DOWN A PATH BY WALKING

Because the route a design project will take is always unclear, and there are no fixed ways to reach a solution, you can do little else than improvise your way to a solution. In terms of a Zen metaphor, you are laying down a path by walking.

The path that this improvisation takes can be based on rational considerations, but often you only have your intuition to guide you. This intuition is a 'feeling' for a direction, but that doesn't mean that it is just an emotional influence. It is based on earlier experiences. In that sense, it need not be irrational either. But it is a vague kind of knowledge, which is hard to capture and make explicit.

Intuition plays a role in all human behaviour. Much of what we think just pops up in our head. Of course, we also reason logically from problem to solution and there are stretches of reasoning where the mind works like a machine, moving through a problem methodically, step by step. But those times seem to be the exception, not the rule. Often we intuitively reach a solution and construct an explanation (rationalisation) afterward.

In design, you need both intuition and reasoning: these two fundamentally dissimilar ways of thinking are combined within every design project. For me, that is part of the attraction of being a designer. It makes designing fascinating, but difficult.

PLATYPUS

Design is often seen as a combination of two ways of thinking, a mixture of problem solving and creativity. We have to creatively develop a design, but this creativity is not completely unrestricted. We have to develop the *right* design, one that solves the problems of the company and the user. This combination of different thinking styles of problem solving and creativity doesn't mean that design is necessarily a schizophrenic occupation. It just means that design is somewhat at odds with the normal ways in which we classify and understand the world.

Maybe a designer can be compared to a duck-billed platypus: this animal, with its duck's beak, webbed feet, furry coat and the habit of producing eggs is always talked about in biology as a 'bizarre phenomenon', an 'anomaly'. Yet, it is only a biological anomaly because the biologists made it so. It is only strange because it doesn't fit neatly into their preconceived view of what a mammal should be. Luckily, the duck-billed platypuses themselves don't seem to be particularly bothered by the way people talk about them. They go about their business like any animal, paddling from pool to pool in their ecological niche.

So, design is a blend of thinking styles. But these are so intimately connected in a design project that, as a designer, you fluently flow from one to the other. That may seem odd to other people, but not to us.

THROWNNESS

A designer is not just working on a design problem, he is *thrown* into a design *situation*. The notion of 'Thrownness' describes the predicament of living in an unstable present.

The activity of 'chairing a meeting' is often used to illustrate this:

When chairing a meeting, you are in a situation that:
- *you cannot avoid acting (doing nothing is also an action).*
- *you cannot step back and reflect on your actions.*
- *the effects of actions cannot be predicted.*
- *you do not have a stable representation of the situation.*
- *every representation you have of 'the situation' is an interpretation.*
- *you cannot be neutral, you are creating the situation you're in.*

This certainly applies to many everyday situations, including design. The point is that when you are designing, you are inside a design process (thrown into the design situation), and not always in the position to consider it critically and rationally. Using your intuition is an essential part of being inside a design situation.

To balance and guide this intuitive side of design, it is sometimes necessary to briefly step out of your design situation, and look critically and rationally at what you are doing. Step back, and look at the bigger picture to see if you are still heading in the right direction.

MR. HEIDEGGER

The notion of 'Thrownness' was coined by the German philosopher Martin Heidegger, as part of a grand programme to explain the world in terms of how we experience it.

What do you experience when you are designing? Most of the time, you are within a flow of consciousness, more or less intuitively following patterns of reasoning. You follow the stream until it stops leading anywhere useful, and peters out. It is only when the reasoning flow breaks down that you become aware of the wider context around what you are doing. It is as if you wake up. Then you have to decide what to do next.

Heidegger's standard example is of using a hammer to drive a nail into the wall. You never think about the hammer, you just pick it up and start hammering. It naturally acts as an extension of your body. The only time you think about the hammer is when it breaks. Suddenly, the whole construction of the object becomes present in your mind in a way that it wasn't before. And if the hammer can't be repaired right away, you might start looking at other objects nearby to see which of them could serve as a hammer. Suddenly you notice their weight, hardness, solidity and possible ease of handling.

The same notion is true for design. You are deeply engrossed in exploring a particular path towards a solution, oblivious of anything else.
The moment a reasoning track comes to a dead end, a wider reality breaks through, and you have to step back and choose a new direction. You often do this by developing alternative routes (for instance, developing different concepts) to try out. You start following them, and some of these experiments might again lead nowhere, but others will succeed.

ABOUT DESIGN
EDUCATION

LEARNING BY DOING

Most design curricula are based upon learning-by-doing. Design schools build their curriculum around design projects which take roughly 50% of the students' time. The other 50% is spent on lectures and skill-related exercises. The learning-by-doing method has many advantages: it provides the student with a rich learning environment that mirrors the design problems they will encounter in practice, and it encourages the development of a personal style. It is rooted in the great tradition of art and craft education, based on a fruitful, personal master-pupil relationship.

Unfortunately, this system is under pressure. Our design schools are growing faster than their financing, while this system of design exercises and tutors is very labour-intensive. Many schools have started 'efficiency drives' by simply cutting the number of hours a staff member may spend with a student. But this is a dangerous step – there must be a tutoring level that is critical, below which the whole system effectively collapses. The holistic and implicit nature of the learning system makes this critical level hard to judge. To perceive this minimal level, you should not – as people normally do – look at the number of good or excellent students that a school delivers: they tend to already be good students when they come in. They don't need a lot of tutoring, only some facilities and the environment to learn. The real symptom that indicates a system collapse is when the mediocre students, who would have become reasonable designers if the system had supported them, begin to fall behind. A better route towards greater efficiency is not to cut the number of tutoring hours, but to make the design exercises shorter and less holistic, more directed toward specific learning goals. This would eliminate some of the unnecessary repetition in design study projects. However, this approach requires a very clear picture of what designing is, and what specific species of designer we want to train.

There is an element of intellectual laziness in a curriculum founded on the idea of 'give them design projects, and they will learn to be a designer'. We cannot afford this anymore, we need to professionalise our design schools by making the design curriculum better aimed and more explicit.

REFLECTION

Design schools base their curriculum on the idea that design is something that must be learned, not taught. When you experience designing and you reflect upon those experiences, you will pick up what design is and how to do it.

This assumes that you are to be able to reflect, to think critically, about what you are doing. This is crucial. If you cannot reflect on your work, the whole educational system collapses, and you might just get through your study projects by trial and error. The design school will often ask you to reflect explicitly, and be able to communicate your thoughts to your tutors. This is quite a tall order. It requires design students (remember, we are talking about 18 year-olds here) to be aware of their design experiences, to be able to write them down explicitly, to select the most relevant ones and find patterns in them, and to then reflect upon these by considering the 'how' and the 'why'. This reflection has again to be put into words, and to be accompanied by ideas for a new course of action for the next project ...!

And we know that it is already difficult for experienced designers to really learn from their design projects. Design projects tend to be so different that it is hard to accumulate knowledge, to take things you learned from one project into the next. The professionals have a lot of trouble with this, and yet we expect students to do so right away.

Because explicit reflection is so hard, designers tend to avoid it by telling each other stories of design projects instead. These stories can evoke the design situation and illustrate the course of a design project quite vividly, allowing you to implicitly relate and compare the story with your own experience, and to learn from them. This is also reflection, but in a more implicit way. You can never hear enough design stories. It is always nice to learn from other designers' mistakes, so that you might not have to make quite so many yourself.

THE TUTORING DILEMMA

The quality of the education in a project based, learning-by-doing, master-pupil model of design education depends heavily on the qualities of the master or tutor. Typically design schools tend to hire experienced designers, because they bring in fresh skills and current trends from the world of design practice.

But this poses some problems. Being a tutor is playing a very specific role which doesn't correspond very well with the normal behaviour of a designer in practice. Designers from practice are typically very eager to solve the problem a student lays before them, and to help the student get a wonderful design by the end of the project. But of course, student's designs are not as important as their learning process. This means that in the role of tutor, you should not say everything that comes into your 'designer's mind'. You must often let the students make the mistakes they are heading for, confront them with those mistakes and then help them reach a different solution. You do not help them learn by solving their problems for them, although that may make both the student and tutor feel good.

What I find most difficult is not answering all their questions. It can be frustrating, especially if you are also the one who must judge the result of the design exercise. Students want clarity from you, not just about the goals of the design exercise, but also about the direction they should take to solve it. And yet they should not get it from you.

It is hard to be placed in a role where you cannot give a straight answer.

THE COACH AND THE JUDGE

Coaching design students is a subtle game of listening and criticising, encouraging and guiding, coming up with examples, fishing for ideas and delivering the occasional stern remark.

A good coach does all of this based on a real relationship of trust with the student. The student should feel that the tutor is actually working on his behalf, and the coach should feel that he is being taken seriously. The stronger this bond of trust, the better the project will go.

However, this bond of trust can feel incredibly awkward when it comes to the final stage of the project, when the coach has to judge the quality of the design work. It is then that the friendly and encouraging mentor suddenly becomes an exacting representative of The School. Often this about-face is felt keenly by the student as a betrayal of the trust that they have built together. The coach is not happy either: he watches a rift appear where once there was solidarity. After judgment has been passed both parties have a hangover, and go their separate ways. They avoid contact as much as possible, except for some vague gestures of greeting when they happen to see each other in the corridor.

This transformation from coach to judge is an unavoidable part of any design curriculum. Many good teachers are unhappy with this situation, and solve the problem by maintaining a mentoring tone during their assessment of the student. They are too nice – it is in the interest of the student to get a sharp and clear judgment, well supported but possibly quite harsh.

What I tend to do is let the student know a couple of weeks before the end of the project that we will be on opposite sides for a while. That the student will have to prove his/her quality to me from now on – a declaration of war, as it were. I always hope that by doing this explicitly it will be possible to re-establish the bond of trust later. Sometimes this works. But it is always difficult.

NAIVE DESIGN

Everyone designs, and everyday 'design' can involve pretty complicated objects. Putting together holiday plans has all the hallmarks of a serious design process: starting out with ambitious goals, you gather information and create alternatives, on the basis of which you negotiate with your travelling companions. It takes quite a bit of shuttling between problem and solution before everybody is satisfied with the final plans.

So any student beginning design school can already design something. But it is difficult to transcend that level of naive design ability. Most design assignments in the first years are so simple that students do not need much more than a naive style to get through them. These design exercises become more difficult because they require ever more knowledge, but they do not require a more sophisticated way of working.

This actually creates a dilemma about the teaching of design models and methods. When you present them early on in their study, students have no use for them yet. You are just making design more difficult (and less fun) by explaining design methods. To students, those methods are just complicated solutions to problems they have never encountered. And if you force students to work according to a method, the absurdity of the heavy-handed model will pitch them against design theory forever. However, if you take the alternative route and introduce design methods at the end of their studies when they start to really need them, the students will have developed all kinds of unfortunate design habits that they then have to unlearn.

A solution to this dilemma has been to teach students a strong design method in the first years, implicitly woven into their design assignments. And then, in the final year of study, to offer a course to reflect on design and design methods, challenging the students to develop their own way of working. The first sessions of that course are dedicated to evaluating the pros and cons of the design methods they have been using. The amount of frustration which is unleashed is positively frightening.

But after that, they are ready to develop their own way of working.

ABSOLUTE BEGINNERS

When you start on the long road towards becoming a designer, you already have developed opinions about what good design is, and what kind of designs you want to create. These opinions are superficial and are often based on a gut reaction to the shape of a design you like, without having any idea of the thoughts and considerations that led to it: *'I want to make something like that!'*

At the start of any design education, these opinions have to be broken down, which can be quite a struggle. The fact that the new students do not know what considerations lie at the root of the designs they like, and have not yet learnt to think about these issues, often just contributes to the strength of their conviction.

Most design schools go for a kind of shock therapy: they plunge the students into a couple of short, intense design projects where the students encounter the limits of their own design abilities, and hopefully draw the conclusion that they might have something to learn after all. A softer approach is to show many examples of design where it can be demonstrated that nothing is black-and-white, and that one can reason and discuss the merits of a design in great detail.

At the Architecture faculty of Sheffield University the staff has developed an interesting assignment to press home this point: in the first week of their studies, the new students are asked to describe the house their parents live in. After a year they are asked to do this again, and discuss the latter description with their parents. Not only will the second description be much longer than the first, it will also be expressed in terminology that the parents will find very hard to understand. Learning to become a designer involves adopting the language in which designs can be thought about, described and discussed.

THE WRONG IDEA

It is a common misconception that the most important thing in designing is to have a good idea. People do not seem to realise that ideas are only the *basis* of a design.

You see this often in design education: a student presents his work at an early stage in the project, and it looks good. Some thought has been put into the project, there are traces of originality in the ideas that were generated. The quality of the design work is usually a bit patchy, but if the student continues in this way a good design will be delivered. As a tutor, you help the student choose a core idea to work on and encourage the student by expressing your happiness with their progress... A couple of weeks later the student presents the end result of the project, which is really disappointing. In the run up to the end presentation the idea has been visualised beautifully, but it has not been developed at all. There has been no critical consideration of the qualities and drawbacks of the idea, which is when the struggle to develop the idea into a design really begins. ('Why develop the idea further? The tutor said he likes it.') The student apparently thinks that the basic idea IS the final design. This is a worrying fundamental mistake: what is missing is the real design work.

With the help of some creativity techniques and a bit of luck everybody can generate nice ideas – you do not need to be a designer for that. The strength of a designer lies in his/her ability to develop ideas into a good design. That is where their core quality lies: single ideas are seldom groundbreakingly original, it is through the combination and integration of ideas that one develops inimitable designs of great complexity and enduring quality. Those designs might be deceptively simple, but this simplicity hides a mountain of ideas and decisions that make the design rich and sophisticated in its appeal.

Educating the student to navigate in this complicated concept development activity should be the core of any design curriculum. But many design schools seem to take the easy route: a single idea presented in a gripping image is considered to be acceptable. I would say that this is not a design education at all, because it fails to address the core effort of the design profession.

LEARNING INTEGRATION

A considerable part of the art of design has to do with integration, with combining the needs of all the stakeholders into a design that addresses all aspects of the product.

How do you learn this difficult process of integration? The ability to integrate is based on a very complex kind of implicit know-how that can only be picked up by doing projects and being tutored. Only a tutor that is involved in the project can explain whether the way you are approaching a particular problem is promising, or propose that you try a different route. In this crucial area of design education, everything depends on the tutors.

The trouble is that good tutors are hard to find, and design schools are tempted to push people with little design experience into the role of design tutor. Quite a few of them do a really good job, coaching the students on many relevant aspects of design. But unfortunately, they lack this implicit knowledge about integration, about how to tackle a problem, which only comes from years and years of design practice. The inexperienced tutors tend to teach design more or less by the book – but this implicit, practice-focussed knowledge of how to approach the problem of integration is not *in* the book.

THE UNSURE

As a tutor, your task is to help all kinds of students become designers, which sometimes gives you vexing problems. For instance, what can you do about a student that is just very uncertain?

In tutoring an insecure student, you quickly get into all sorts of vicious circles. They tend to cling to the safety of their first idea. Criticising the student for being inflexible by not letting go of their initial idea, makes the student even more unsure, and more dependent on the tutor... If you go down that road, you end up with students who won't dare to go into the world after their study. And agoraphobia is not a good trait for a designer. Maybe it is better to be very diplomatic, and hum approvingly over the first idea. But then you create the impression that it's a good idea when it is not.

This calls for a solution at a different level. Confidence needs to be based on something, and that can be almost anything. Some students draw really well, others are good problem solvers, others are socially adept. Find a student's strong point, that can be used to stimulate a wider development, to build a basis for a broader confidence.

If that doesn't work or such a core competence is hard to find, as a tutor you can only wait for other things in the student's life which could create an opening. Just keep on tutoring, and keep repeating that you are criticising the work, not the person. This process can take so long that students can be at the end of their studies before their confidence is really at a high enough level to start learning. You just have to hope that their level of confidence will support further development in practice.

However, these people are extremely vulnerable in their first job. If they are not handled with care, they might really get hurt. And the outside world can be a mean place.

THE RIGHT PERSON, AT THE RIGHT TIME

If you are really lucky, you'll encounter one good design tutor during your four or five years in design school. The right person, at the right time.

Becoming a designer is not a gradual process, it goes in leaps and bounds. You can be stuck in a certain way of working for quite a long time, before you develop a new understanding of the issues confronting you and develop a new way of designing for yourself. It is at these critical moments that you need a tutor who understands your predicament in a way that you cannot even verbalise yet, and that really understands you as a person.

For design tutors, these are the trickiest situations to navigate. Some students will only build up real understanding of how they could approach design differently by coming up with the solution themselves. In that case, the tutor just needs to feed the process a little bit and stay out of the way as much as possible. Other students need a well-aimed impulse (kick) to get them thinking in the right direction. The subtle art of being a design tutor lies in the ability to identify and adopt the most productive strategy at these critical moments in the development of a design student. That can be very difficult, especially when you are confronted with a student whose psychological makeup is unlike your own. Big character differences between student and tutor can easily lead to a breakdown in communication at this crucial point in time, and then the learning opportunity is lost.

A design tutor is only human, and nobody can be a good mentor to all students. Both the student and the tutor need quite a bit of luck to come together at the right time.

THE WRONG THING TO SAY

Although design schools tend to work largely on a project-basis, there are moments when it is really more efficient to address a crowd of students to explain some theory. At least, that is what the experts say – but I am not so sure. It sounds efficient, but efficiency is useless when what you do is actually ineffective.

One of the problems of this form of classroom teaching is the diversity of design students. Try to devise a lecture that will inform and inspire a classroom population of technically oriented inventors, pragmatic problem solvers, autonomous furniture designers and potential visionary artists, all mixed together and staring at you. Anything you say will be completely beside the point for a good part of your audience. Or worse, it could be counterproductive, even harmful.

That awful feeling gets to me now and then when I explain the classic phase models of the structure of design processes (orientation – analysis – synthesis – testing – deciding, as you know) to a group of unsuspecting students. It will always be the unsure and the anxious, those who need to loosen up by tackling wildly creative challenges, who will end up limiting themselves more than ever by clinging to a process structure for dear life. And the creatively confused talents, who could use a bit of a structure here and there to make sure that they will achieve more progress in their concept development (those who, through lack of structure, will always run out of time and produce disappointing concepts as a result), will naturally turn away from a lecture about process structure and ignore it completely...

UNREAL DESIGN

Design schools want to prepare their students well for design practice. That is why educators go to great effort to develop 'realistic' design projects. But this kind of realism is a bit of a joke – it does not go very far, really.

The main problem with this 'realistic' approach is at the very beginning of a design project, where students are given a 'design problem'. In the real world, there are no 'design problems'. Real-world design projects emerge from a subtle game of discussion and negotiation that is played after the initial client contact. It can take ages before the decision to start defining a design assignment is even taken. In this pre-project phase the designer and the client get to know each other, and they slowly and gradually build the trust that is necessary for a fruitful cooperation... What a difference from the educational setting!

Pure fear of ambiguity drives the tutors to begin a design project with a predefined brief on two A4's. In this way the student misses the all-important pre-design project phase.

And that has dire consequences: the complete inability to deal with the pre-design phase is the first thing that students will encounter when they enter design practice. They do not even know that this phase exists, let alone knowing what is expected of them in terms of the game that needs to be played. This ignorance renders them completely powerless. In the worst case, the young designer will just ask the client for a well-defined design assignment, which rules out any chance of contributing to the all-important development of the design problem.

The creation of the design problem is a crucial design activity because it is in developing the design problem that you question the old assumptions a client might have, create the freedom you need as a designer, and establish your position as a trusted partner in the scary adventure of innovation. Failure to develop the design problem with the client precludes any possibility for real innovation.

THE GUY FROM PRACTICE

There is always pressure put on design schools by industry to ensure that design training connects well with the daily practice of the design world. Of course, schools are sensitive to this argument, and they try to foster this continuity by hiring designers from practice to tutor design students, usually for one day a week. The idea is that these designers from practice can tell the students about the daily struggle of real design from first-hand experience. What could be a better way to connect to practice?

The results are pretty discouraging – if anything, the gap between design schools and practice seems to have increased rather than been diminished by hiring more practicing designers. So much so that Gabriela Goldschmidt, eminent design researcher, decided to look into this by interviewing the guys from practice and the students they tutor.

And what seems to be case? It turns out that the practicing designers tend to enjoy their work at the design school, precisely because it gives them the opportunity to get away from the daily struggle of real-life commercial work. Therefore, they seize the opportunity to talk about design in the most general and abstract terms, painting the broadest possible narrative vistas, talking about design as an ephemeral phenomenon, rather than as a profession. They like to talk about anything but the drudgery and problems of daily design work.

And the students? They desperately want to hear the real-life experience that their tutors do not want to talk about.

OUTSTANDING DESIGNERS

People generally agree that Talent is important in a designer. By Talent, they mean something magical: an inborn gift of achievement. A present from Mother Nature.

We like such myths. But the down side of this myth is, of course, that you either have Talent, or you don't. If Mother Nature passed you by when you were born, you are out of luck. That is a stumbling block, if ever there was one, for people who are interested in improving design education: if quality depends on an innate gift, design schools will have very little effect. Luckily, there are few people within the 'nature versus nurture' debate that still defend this extreme position. There is some consensus that even a natural talent needs a good environment in order to develop. So schools become important again.

But how do schools deal with their really talented students?

I get the impression that most schools don't really consider this, and that opportunities might be lost. The talented ones are squeezed through the same broad schooling as all the other students, whether they need it or not. You sometimes see talented students go astray because of this. The bigger talents often have an element of danger in them, something absolute, an all-or-nothing monomaniacal streak. They are so focussed on what they strongly want and what they really can do very well, that any call for flexibility is lost upon them. Great talents tend to not do so well in school. They are self-propelled and easily collide with any system, be it their school or the outside world.

It is important for design schools to recognise these talents and to give some extra attention while guiding them. Not to start another 'elite design school', but just because these people need some extra care.

LEVELS OF EXCELLENCE

What does it mean to be good at your profession?

Scott McCloud provides something of an answer for the creators of cartoon art. He holds that you can practice your profession on several levels. His idea is that you move through these levels in your development as a cartoonist. He divides this development into six stages.

You first work on the Surface, which means that you can just make a drawing that looks professional. You then move to the level of learning the Craft. From there you begin to be creative on a Structural level. The best cartoonists then move on to develop a new Idiom with their art, or even to change the Form of the medium. The very greatest renew the basic Idea of the artform.

These levels involve different kinds of creativity, knowledge and skills.

It is hard to map these levels one to one onto the design fields as we know them, but the whole idea is very recognizable. One of the nicest things in teaching design is to see students advance from one level to the next. Learning to be a designer is not a smooth process at all, it moves in fits and starts. It can be extremely frustrating to laboriously achieve competence in one level, without visibly moving forward ... but when you manage to reach a new level, a new world literally opens up to you. It is a real breakthrough.

As a tutor, this is very nice to witness. You can feel something is about to happen when the student starts producing work that is a lot better or deeper than the student realises. You then spend considerable time explaining to the student what is so good about his/her own idea. These are strange conversations: the tutor is very enthusiastic, and the student is very confused. In nine out of ten cases the student really doesn't understand what the tutor is talking about, and will most likely blow the whole idea later on in the project. But sometimes it just clicks, and those are fascinating moments. The birth of a designer. As a tutor, you feel you have gained a colleague to discuss your profession with – an equal.

SNOWBALLING

We do not really know how some students grow to become excellent designers. But we do know that this rise to excellence is not a gradual process. The design abilities of some students can get to some mysterious turning point, and after that they just start snowballing.

This defining moment has to do with a change in attitude, more than anything else. It is as if a student suddenly wakes up to the world. The student begins to actively engage in the world around him, which sparks off a nonstop learning process. They immediately relate everything they see to their design work. Compared to this 'learning from the world' any school is just an artificial environment. A weak substitute for all the graphics, technology, products and architecture that surround us 24 hours a day.

But how can we encourage this snowballing of design ability? We do not know. What we do know is that you have to be careful, in any design curriculum, not to smother these possible breakthroughs with an avalanche of well-meant design knowledge. There should be time and opportunity for students to get out into the world. Snowballing will often start outside the regular design curriculum in a trainee situation. A traineeship can be stimulating, in an exciting environment with lots of inspiration and new-found freedom. Just what they need. Students who have experienced this expansion of their abilities in a traineeship often clash with their own design schools when they return to finish their studies. Quite rightly so. They have moved beyond the discipline that is imposed in a school, and are quite capable of growing further by themselves.

'A method, in the realm of the mind, can be compared to a crutch. The true thinker walks free.' In training designers, we should take care not to impose the use of crutches on people who would have been able to walk by themselves.

THE EVOLUTION OF A DESIGNER

If we look at other professional fields, we find some models dealing with the development of expertise that might be helpful in understanding the evolution of our own strange species. The philosopher Hubert Dreyfus distinguishes six distinct levels of expertise, corresponding with six ways of perceiving, interpreting, structuring and solving problems.

A *novice* designer will consider the objective features of a situation, as they are pointed out by experts, and will follow strict rules ('the rules of the game') to tackle the design problem. For the *advanced beginner*, situational aspects are important ('what to do when?'). Therefore, the advanced beginner is sensitive to exceptions to the 'hard' rules of the novice. Maxims are used for guidance through the complex problem situation. A *competent* designer works in a radically different way, choosing a plan to achieve certain goals – thereby actively shaping the design situation. The *expert designer* responds to a specific design situation intuitively, on the basis of a vast experience. There is no explicit problem solving and reasoning that can be distinguished at this level - the expert can deal with any problem in his/her domain in a fluent manner. With the next level, the *master*, a new uneasiness creeps in. The master sees the ways of working that the expert designer uses not as natural but as contingent. A master will dwell on the reasons behind successes and failures, and perform experiments in practice. Thus the master adds new knowledge and paradigms to the professional field. Finally, the *visionary* consciously strives to extend the domain in which he/she works. They envision new ways things could be, define the issues and open new worlds. A visionary is likely to operate on the margins of a domain, seeking out marginal practices that hold promise for the future.

These levels of expertise can spark immediate recognition in designers. Somehow, you get the feeling that you know these people. Nonetheless, a couple of qualifications are in order: the first one is that the model does not mean to describe a complete person. We switch between these levels of expertise all the time (speaking for myself: I feel like an expert in Form giving, but I am a novice in Electronics – so I would need an expert to point out what formulas I need to use). Secondly, one level is not necessarily better than the other in a given situation. Perhaps it would be better to talk about varieties of design thinking, rather than levels of design expertise.

THE CULT OF THE DESIGN CONCEPT

When the circumstances are just right, some designers can develop into visionary conceptual thinkers. They can create ideas or designs that take the world by surprise, creating a quantum leap in our collective consciousness. That is something grand, fantastic and wonderful. But the magic does not happen very often, and my experiences in design education tell me that you probably cannot aim for it directly. Actually, the only way to make sure that such a conceptual leap will *not* happen is to strive for it directly, because then your design creativity cramps up...

It worries me when I see many design schools adopt the achievement of revolutionary conceptual leaps as the sole aim and model for their students. In adopting this impossible goal they could be pointing many students in the wrong direction, away from the things that they *could* achieve. There is also an element of unfairness in saddling students with such unattainable goals: you are asking absolute beginners to manifest a maturity that they cannot yet have. If you visit the graduation shows of these schools you can see how the students have wrestled to respond to these overblown expectations in any way they could. They desperately want to come up with a conceptual breakthrough in all their projects. And the result of this burden is that they, in the end, follow the master in a most slavish way, much more slavishly than if they had been allowed to build up their own work without having to be a groundbreaking genius all the time. They end up being unduly influenced by their masters, what else can they do? They cannot produce a deep vision about the profession themselves, so they desperately hold on to someone who will *tell* them what is interesting and new.

These graduation exhibitions can be heartbreaking. Year after year you see students producing bland variants of the master's work, accompanied by a pretentious story that claims an earth-shattering originality.

THE IMAGE OF THE DESIGN PROFESSION

Most people just beginning their design education have no idea what awaits them. Their knowledge of design is based on the image that the media paints of our profession. Success stories, full of creative geniuses who scribble wonderful ideas while staring into the distant future. Alternatively, there are the 'home improvement' programmes where an obviously rich 'successful designer' with a great nimbus of wavy hair uses a bag of cheap design tricks to the admiration of all.

These images are an incredibly weak basis for the choice of a design career. Design is fascinating, exhilarating, but also a very demanding profession – it is something that you have to embrace completely. I would not go so far as to say it is a calling, but it has some of those elements.

The design sector suffers dearly from the image that is spread by the media. The culture of easy success stories attracts people to the design profession who are completely unsuitable for the job – being a designer involves working very very hard. If you are only in it for the glowing image of public success and are not prepared to do what it takes to become a really good designer, you might as well get out now. This wretched image of easy and superficial success also makes it hard for real designers to get the recognition, trust and esteem that they are entitled to. You are just not taken very seriously when people mentally class you with all of those clowns from television. Something must be done. It would actually be really helpful if the designers who are interviewed by the media were to be a bit more honest and curtail their vanity. Of course it is tempting to pretend that this amazing design was created effortlessly, and play down the amount of hard work that went into it. The more you talk about the work, the less of a genius you are. But we need to find ways of projecting a more realistic image of what we do, if only because the 90% of design work that nobody ever talks about in the media is also the core substance of design, the work that makes design the challenging, complex and fascinating profession it is.

LIMITS OF AN EDUCATION

People often worry whether a design school can prepare you well for design practice. My answer would be: of course not. It can't, for several reasons.

First of all, design is much too broad a subject, and all design schools aim their education at enormous sections within the design field. So you end up training students that will go off into many different directions. This means that in the first few years of their studies you can only teach them the basics of 'design' in general, leaving one or two years to train them in the specific area of their choice. That is not much time. Students are not 'finished' after four or five years, and will always experience a mismatch between what they have learnt and what their first job requires from them.

A second reason for the perceived rift between education and practice really lies in the perception itself. People expect more from their education than it can ever provide. A study is just a basis, a foundation for further learning. Educational specialists estimate that it takes at least ten years to become really good at your profession – the first four or five are spent studying, and the rest you must learn in practice. Your first jobs are probably more crucial to your development as a designer than your time in school. And after that, well, you never stop learning.

The whole question of whether 'the school' prepares a student for 'design practice' cannot really be answered in these general terms. 'The school' and 'design practice' don't exist: the question is whether your education forms a foundation for developing the kind of design practice that suits *you*. This relieves much of the schools' responsibility and transfers it to the shoulders of the student. Students need to find out who they are, what kind of design area suits them, and devise their own training. The quality of a design school is therefore, to a large extent, determined by its ability to feed and assist this development.

NIGHTMARES

In this book, I keep emphasizing the importance of case studies and stories about design. Unfortunately, these stories are not easy to find.

Most anecdotes and books about design are just smooth presentations of wonderful projects. They only seem to be written to project the ego of the designer, declaring how wonderfully clever he is. They help perpetuate myths about creativity and design that are not only unhelpful to design students, but in my opinion positively damaging. We suffer from this design cult.

As a design educator, I constantly have to delve into my own design experience to come up with the right stories to illustrate the point I want to make. What we need are these 'inside' accounts about actual design practice, including the difficulties and failures that are part and parcel of being a designer. There is so much to be learned from such stories, they are invaluable.

The association of Dutch designers once organised a 'Design Horror Night' (on Friday the 13th), in which designers came together to present their worst design experiences. The really bad projects, the utter failures, and the most awful products ever made by well-meaning designers. Hilarious and wonderful, but always a bit too close to home.

BEING A DESIGNER

ON

DESIGNERS

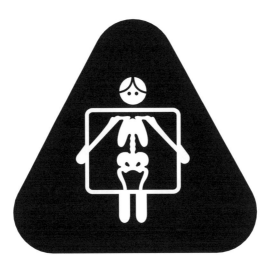

THE DESIGN ABILITY

What abilities and skills do you need to be a designer?

We have seen that naive design is similar to common sense reasoning and is something that most people can do. But what do we expect professional designers to be good at?

Nigel Cross (design researcher and educator) has been focussing on these questions, and has made a list of eight core design abilities that all designers must have. According to him, designers must have the ability to: (1) produce novel, unexpected solutions by (2) applying imagination and constructive forethought to practical problems, (3) using drawings and other modelling media as means of problem solving. In doing this, they need to be able to (4) deal with uncertainty and decision making on the basis of limited information, (5) resolve ill-defined, 'wicked' problems by (6) adopting solution-focussing strategies, (7) employing productive/ creative thinking and (8) using graphic or spatial modelling media.

This is an impressive list with a wide range of necessary skills. Other such lists exist which define design in even wider terms, and include competencies like 'integrating technologies', 'social and cultural awareness' and 'self directed learning'. These inventories of design abilities are important, because they are used to set design education curriculums, and by implication, define the kind of designer that is being trained in a design school.

Some of these abilities can be learned or taught in a fairly straightforward way. There are drawing courses and clever tricks to stimulate creative thinking. If you take the courses and apply the techniques, you can become quite proficient. Unfortunately, not all of these basic design abilities can be learned easily. Some design abilities are very complicated ('resolving wicked problems'). It is even hard to imagine how one could develop such skills at all, or they are deeply rooted in the personality of a designer ('dealing with uncertainty'). They defy education, but could instead be used to select students applying for design courses. If we are sure that these are the essential qualifications, that is.

PSYCHOLOGY OF DESIGN

We know that design is a complicated profession, but if design ability depends upon the personality or psyche of the designer, we need to see if psychology can help us understand these 'deeper' roots of designership.

A recent trend in psychology, initiated by Howard Gardner, supposes that there is not just one kind of intelligence, but that there are several, relatively autonomous human intellectual faculties. They discern six forms of intelligence: linguistic, logical/mathematical, spatial, musical, bodily/kinaesthetic and personal.
The core design skills discussed before seem to require all six forms of intelligence. This would mean that design is a broad, all encompassing activity that doesn't require extreme intelligence in any of the six varieties, but rather a combination of these intelligences. This is a bit different from many other professions, which clearly use only one intelligence, or perhaps, a combination of two.

This makes design hard to place for other people. There is something obscure about the design ability if it is this complex brew of traits. This could also explain the many species of designers. The designers I know are a very diverse bunch of people, who could be characterised as 'the entrepreneur', 'the artist', 'the logician', 'the pragmatist', etc. These designers naturally take on various roles in design teams, and in a way, their diversity is a good reason in itself to prefer designing in teams. You need all kinds of design abilities to achieve an interesting design.

There have been experiments at Stanford University to maximize the personality differences when assembling a design team (they used the Meyers-Briggs type indicator to test the students). In that situation, each of the team members were innovative or extreme in one or more of the six forms of intelligence, while they shared a broad common background based on their education. The design teams turned out to be very successful.

PERSONAL AGENDA

There are many reasons for becoming a designer. Some people want to see their ideas turned into reality, others become designers because they see it as a way to express their innermost selves, or are motivated by higher ideals (to make the world a better place). In fact, all reasons are valid, as long as they are strongly felt and personal. However, some of these motivations may be more prone to frustration than others.

Design schools are not easy, and the students whose inspiration is too weak will not make it. In any crop of first year design students, there are a few who just chose design because they were attracted to the visual aspect of it, and see it as a 'nice' study. This is seldom enough to muster the resolve to finish.

Design schools look deceptively innocent, in a 'back to kindergarten' kind of way. But students soon discover that becoming a designer is hard work: the constant flow of design assignments is, by itself, quite enough to fill your days to overflowing. If you don't apply yourself and work hard on these design assignments you can still probably get by, but you will not learn much, and the whole study becomes pointless.

And becoming a design professional is not a comfortable process either. It involves intense personal development. You have to be able to deal with criticism of work that is close to your heart since you had put a lot of time, effort and ideas into it. You have to present and defend your own opinions about design. It is not the kind of study where you can safely hide behind books and are only judged by exam results. There is nothing anonymous about becoming a designer. A lack of enthusiasm will sooner or later come to the surface and make it that much harder.

On the other hand, if you chose right in opting for design, you will get a broad education where you learn to keep learning and to enjoy confrontations that will aid your personal development. This is the kind of quality that the artist Joseph Beuys referred to when he was asked about how he taught his students: *'I try to teach (painting) in such a way that if one of my students later decides to become a plumber, he will be a good plumber.'*

UNCERTAINTY

The outstanding structural engineering designer Ted Happold said: *'I really have, perhaps, one real talent – that is that I don't mind at all living in an area of total uncertainty.'*

This is a sobering thought for the people who drive across his bridges.

What does it take to be a good designer? Are there any personality traits that really help or hinder a designer's development? At my university, we explored these questions by observing design students as they worked on a task and interviewed them about their design behaviour. It turned out that the students who came up with the worst designs all had one trait in common: they had come up with a solution right away, because they felt nervous without any design proposal.

This makes you realise that design is a very risky profession. As a designer, you work on a complex design problem, possibly for months on end, without really knowing for sure that you will succeed in creating a satisfying solution. This generates a certain tension, a restlessness. It is a bit like tightrope walking. Some people naturally like this creative tension, and are attracted to it. These are not just thrill seekers – good designers use this tension as a source of energy, to make something special which they couldn't have done in a more relaxed situation.

But this kind of tension doesn't agree with everyone. Some like a safer world. The design students who have what psychologists call a 'low tolerance for uncertainty', tend to concentrate on their first solution and improve on it, instead of going through the uncertainty associated with a complete phase of idea generation. They never get around to producing interesting designs. We all know that initial ideas are often not the best ones.

THE ARROGANCE OF DESIGN

Designers want to create novel and interesting things. Unfortunately, for a design to succeed, they have to work in close cooperation with their employers or clients. Ignore the other parties and your wonderful ideas will never reach the world. There are examples of famous designers (mainly architects) that made a name for themselves on the basis of their design plans alone. It must be sad to win competitions but never build anything.

Working with a client is not always easy. There is something about the role of the designer that is just asking for trouble. This has been aptly put by the architect Denys Lasdun: *'Our job is to give the client, on time and on cost, not what he wants, but what he never DREAMED he wanted – and when he gets it he recognises it as something he wanted all the time.'*

On first reading this may seem a shockingly arrogant statement, yet it should not be dismissed as a personal remark by an obnoxious person. This kind of arrogance is an integral part of design. As a designer, you are not hired to produce the obvious. You have to go beyond the client's or employer's preconceived image of the new design, and employ your specialist knowledge and skills to design something that is better than they could imagine. This way of not precisely doing what you are asked to do may be interpreted as arrogance by those at the other side of the table. So be it. This is the only way to give them value for money. It is all part of being a designer.

To manage this potentially problematic relationship, you must develop the ability to listen closely to the client and discover what he/she really wants. To strive to understand the client better than the client understands himself. Good designers are excellent listeners. The shortcut is to not listen at all, and impose your own goals upon a confused client. Now THAT is arrogant.

DESIGN RATS

The design community tends to have an uneasy relationship with the commercial world in which most designers operate. This is rather strange: designers always say their mission is to create designs that are relevant to the outside world, and that they have taken up the design profession motivated by a burning desire to use their creative talents to make people happy.

However, when this outside world comes walking into the office (say, in the guise of a client, or – worse – a marketeer), to tell designers how their work can be especially relevant to the outside world, many designers shut the door and cover their ears. They fear being constrained by the messages they might receive from beyond their studio door. When it comes to it, these designers apparently love their freedom just a little bit more than they love humbly serving their fellow human beings. The more you think about it, the stranger this becomes: we all know that designing always involves creating things for others – yet many designers tend to be motivated by the fun of designing itself, or by the love for their own creations, and do not seem to want to know too much about the others they are designing for. Is design a schizophrenic profession? Perhaps.

These issues have led to a clear dichotomy within the design community. There is a huge rift in the design world between two species of designers, the 'creative freedom fighters' described above and the more commercially oriented designers. There is no middle ground, and you will never confuse the two types when you meet them: commercially oriented designers look unmistakably different from the creative freedom fighters, they walk differently, they talk differently, and they talk about completely different things. They take their cue from the business world, mimicking their clients by wearing suits and having efficient-looking offices. They enjoy the business game that design also is. They are looked down upon by the creative freedom fighters, who see themselves as the 'real designers', far superior to those 'design rats'. Still, in the harsh reality of a capitalist world order the game of design is also a very commercial one. Ideally, designers should acquire the split personality necessary to work in both worlds, and alternate between 'free' projects and those that have great commercial value.

BEING A DESIGNER

CREATIVE
MINDS

MAGIC AND MYTH

Creativity is often seen as the unique human capacity to think up something new out of nothing. A magical gift that all great creative minds possess. Creativity is surrounded by myths about sudden inspiration, the Eureka moments and 'aha' experiences.

We use the word creativity for anything that we experience as new, when we cannot easily explain where it came from. But when we look at the lives of creative people, we can always see the different threads of knowledge that led to their new discovery. What seems to be needed for a real creative leap, is a single-mindedness and dedication towards solving a problem or making a new development. There is often also some paradox involved in the problem or situation that forces the creative person to search for a new way toward a solution. Their new way is then constructed by combining different ways of thinking. This can lead to a whole new field of discovery to be explored energetically. Some 'creatives' keep searching for new areas of paradox and conflict to repeat this feat, others seem to have stumbled on an area that was ready for a creative leap more or less by accident, as a once in a lifetime experience.

This is a difficult and fascinating process, but not a magical one. Being creative doesn't mean sitting around waiting for a sudden bolt to hit you. It is a pity that the myths surrounding creativity tend to cloud people's view of the work that is necessary to be creative.

DARWIN'S EUREKA THAT NEVER WAS

The idea of the creative leap which suddenly illuminates the mind of its inventor, dates from the middle of the 19th century. Of course, it is hard to say if this is truly how creativity works. There seem to be vague moments at the birth of ideas, which could be described and explained in a number of different ways. The most magical of all, the Eureka experience, is a folk psychology favourite. It is easy to reconstruct an idea's coming to light in a way that confirms this theory.

In his autobiography, Darwin claimed to have created his theory of evolution and natural selection in such a creative flash. He writes that the idea suddenly hit him when he was reading a treatise on human population by Malthus. Luckily for us, we can trace this moment of glory in his original diary of that time, where he dutifully reports having read Malthus. But no Eureka. Just a brief entry. The next day he wrote a much longer piece on the sexual curiosity of primates. Reading Malthus was lost in a host of other books that he was browsing through at the time, and he developed many different ideas to explain the diversity of species that he had encountered in his voyage on the Beagle. If we read the diary carefully we can see that the idea of natural selection slowly dawned upon him.

Darwin's creation of the theories of evolution and natural selection was a gigantic creative step. But there never was that one Eureka moment.

BRAINSTORMING

The most popular creativity technique, brainstorming, aims to 'loosen the mind' to put forward wild associations which might lead to approaching the problem in a different and interesting way.

In a brainstorming session it is important to create an open atmosphere where people feel free to just throw in their ideas and associations. Anything goes, because it might spark some interesting connections. People are encouraged to build upon the ideas of one another, so the chain of thought profits from the various association patterns in the minds of the participants. The one restrictive rule in a brainstorming session is that people are not allowed to criticise each other's ideas. A fresh and mad idea is a brittle thing, that can be dismissed quite easily as being unrealistic or strange. A critical remark will immediately halt the flow of ideas. The whole session aims to get as many ideas as possible, good as well as bad.

Brainstorming is often used in isolation, as a trick to generate new ideas, but used in that way it is of questionable value to a design project. These sessions easily lose direction and might only result in completely unworkable ideas. Brainstorming sessions are really meant to be part of a multi-step process in which ideas are generated and selected. This begins with a special session that focusses on creatively analysing the design problem. This is crucial, because the impulse for innovation is in the assignment. Only assignments with open possibilities which contain some compulsion to make something new, will lead to novelty in the design.

That is why designers always try to meddle with the design problem, and also why design competitions are always won by the designers who did not really stick to the brief.

SITUATED CREATIVITY

In a study I did into the creative behaviour of product designers, there were some issues in the design assignment which, with the extra information provided, could easily be combined into a product idea.

All of the designers picked out these four issues in their exploration of the assignment, amongst the many other issues to which they had to attend. All nine experienced designers combined these same loose bits of information into the same idea, which they then reported as an original idea, a key concept in their solution. The designers were very enthusiastic about their concept, and were convinced that they were going to beat any competitors with this fresh approach. They experienced it as an emotional kick, a real 'aha' event.

It is interesting that they all seemed to think that their idea was original. Indeed it was original, in the sense that it was different from the existing product – it was also original and new to each individual designer. But the re-occurrence of the same idea, independently, in the minds of all nine designers suggests that it might have been an 'easy' step in originality – that certain kinds of information within the problem data brought up similar 'creative' concepts. Ideas are not always as original as they seem. It is worth checking where they came from.

HUMOUR

It is a good sign if you hear laughter coming from a design team. Humour, with its exaggerations and unexpected twists, is a free flowing and loose way of dealing with reality. Looking at the world obliquely can yield fresh and original insights. It allows a designer move away from the ordinary, and to start playing with concepts and ideas.

In a way humour is not unlike design. It is often based upon design-like ways of thinking, such as the use of exaggeration, metaphors or the graphic depiction of a situation in the mind's eye.

However, some kinds of humour are more productive than others. Nihilistic or cynical humour is not usually directly useful in the generation of ideas, but it can perform a really important role in design by allowing the introduction of subjects that would have been taboo if they had been brought up in a more serious mode. The irreverence that is part and parcel of the humoristic mind helps us break out of the box of social conventions, and shows us what possibilities lay beyond the normal, accepted ways of thinking.

'FRESHNESS'

Many students start their design projects by brainstorming, because they are still 'fresh' at that point. They expect this 'freshness' to give them the brilliant ideas that they hope for. Unfortunately it doesn't seem to work that way... Generating ideas based on a minimum of information and with only a vague idea about the problem just leads to naive, uninteresting, or standard solutions. A waste of time.

At the root of this misconception are a few misunderstandings about the nature of idea generation.

First of all, the fact that idea generation works on the basis of free associations does not mean that it is a random process. In idea generation, you must let yourself be inspired by the design problem and all the knowledge that you have built up around it. Only then can you select the ideas that seem to have the greatest potential to create value in the design, and build upon them. So you first need to explore the design problem, getting to know what kinds of values are important for the particular design challenge. Then you build up a rich picture of the design problem, and amass all kinds of knowledge that might be relevant when generating ideas. The richer, the better.

Another misunderstanding has to do with the fear of getting stuck. People tend to assume that the more you know, the harder it is to come up with original solutions. This fear is partly legitimate. 'Design fixation' can happen all too easily. Fortunately, there are tricks to overcome this barrier, for instance by beginning a brainstorming session with a round of 'purging'. Just picking out the obvious ideas, and putting them on paper is often enough to inspire people to surpass them in further brainstorming rounds. The most awful, unproductive idea generation sessions that I participated in were caused by a lack of knowledge about the design problem, not because of an excess.

BEING A DESIGNER

HEAD
HEART
HAND

INVOLVEMENT

It is important to get as close as possible to the subject of the design assignment. Design is a complicated problem solving activity where our first-hand experience, and the intuition that this creates, deeply influences the countless almost implicit decisions you make while designing.

It is a bit pompous to talk about the 'soul' of a design, but the personal involvement of a designer in what he designs is a great source of quality. My own most conscientious designs are some medical equipment I made after helping care for a family member at home. Not the most spectacular designs, but made with a very intimate knowledge of the needs and wants of people in such a situation. No hastily gathered 'research' can beat that.

The real core of a designer's thinking is always based upon his or her engagement and personal concern with the design, which comes most readily from the designer's own direct experiences. Of course, you cannot ask design students and designers to go looking for direct personal experiences for every new design project. But they should try to get into personal contact with people who have been in such a situation, and try to learn from their experiences. We can't remove ourselves too far from direct human experience and still create relevant designs. Head, heart and hand should all be involved in design.

EMPATHY

Empathy is the ability to project your personality into another person, to imagine 'standing in their shoes'. It is as close as we can get to really understanding someone else, and to appreciate what the other person is going through.

The ability to empathise is a real gift for a designer: it enables you to feel what future users of the design will experience. This feat of the imagination yields an incredible amount of information that can be taken into consideration before the design, or even a prototype, is made. It improves a design much more than any token 'usage scenario' or 'user research'.

And empathy can also be a great help in communicating with the stakeholders of the design project, such as the client and the production manager. If you are able to change standpoints, you can become aware of what drives them before a presentation meeting, and get an idea how they are going to react to the design. It might even help you to imagine how such a person sees you, as a designer presenting this design concept. This could help avoid or avert misunderstandings that often seem to accompany design projects. But of course, you should take care not to lose your own point of view in the process.

A third way in which I have seen empathy play a role in design, is that you can imagine that you are your design. Normally it is considered a fallacy to ascribe feelings and emotions to objects, but in design it can be useful to do so. OK, imagine you are your design. Where are you? What do you see? What is around you? Do you feel warm or cold? This provides a lively picture of the situation in which your design will exist. Some design schools and designers act out the use of the design.

To develop this empathic ability, you have to be a very good observer of people, so that you will start imagining what it would be like to be them. Being an avid caricaturist also helps a lot. If there is one lost cause that I would like to champion, it would be teaching caricature drawing in every design school. Most design students are completely oblivious to their fellow human beings, and just design for themselves. They miss a lot.

'THE QUALITY WITHOUT A NAME'

It is surprisingly difficult to pinpoint what constitutes a 'good' design. It has something to do with the way the design enriches our experience, and how we can relate to it.

Creating this kind of value, this human quality, is much more subtle than just making an object that does not break right away. We all know what are considered good examples of design in our particular field, be it a fine building, an excellent machine, product or good graphics. But what makes them intrinsically 'good'? This is a question that brings us closer to the realm of art than we normally are, and maybe nearer than we want to be.

A designer can easily avoid these difficult issues by just making mundane stuff that functions and looks attractive. But we know that there are higher values to aim for, also in design. To make things that people will not only use, but like, and perhaps grow fond of. We know that some designs really affect people, and can be inspiring and moving at the same time.

To achieve this quality, we must aim higher than just functionality or blind self-expression, towards a deeper (more universal) human value. This may sound vague and metaphysical. But I hope you recognise that there is something like Quality with a capital Q. Some objects manage to be intelligently made, practical, and good to relate to. They combine head, heart and hand in a striking fashion.

MOTORCYCLE MAINTENANCE

In 'Zen and the Art of Motorcycle Maintenance', Robert Pirsig describes how he drives through the US on a motorcycle, and how he lovingly keeps resetting the engine to the circumstances, tinkering with it and adjusting it.

He carefully works with his machine to get it just right, and describes the patience it takes as well as the pleasure it gives. Small repairs become creative challenges, and make him fonder and fonder of his own machine. Meanwhile he ponders the meaning of Quality, and the attitude of his fellow travelers toward technology. They see technology as an artificial and alien thing which interferes with people's lives and estranged them from a pristine and happy 'natural' state. They are of course immersed in technology, but hate it and do not know how to deal with it.

Meanwhile, Pirsig adjusts his motorcycle to be in tune with the road and the weather, and enjoys the quality of life you get from being in harmony with your machine.

THINKING TOOLS FOR DESIGNERS

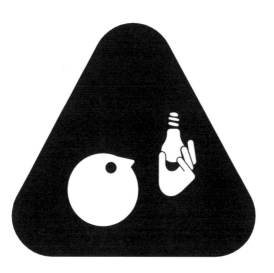

FUNCTIONS

Designers have different thinking tools they can use to attack a design problem. These tools, such as the use of functions, analogies, frames and strategies, all have their specific properties, strengths and weaknesses.

Functions help designers to think about their design problem in more general terms. This opening up of the problem alone can help generate unexpected solutions. Functions thus are an ideal form of 'intermediary' between design problem and solution. Thinking in functions is a natural and almost unavoidable way of thinking when working on a design project. In concentrating on functions, you describe what the design has to do as a list of verbs. And each of these verbs easily evokes many possible objects that could fulfil that function. You can also use functions to analyse a design problem by making a 'function tree'. You start by listing the main function that has to be fulfiled, and break it down into smaller functions that have to be realised in order for the main function to succeed. You end up with layers and layers of functions, branching out from the main function.

Unfortunately, there are also pitfalls in working with functions – one of which has to do with the fact that functions and solutions are often denoted by the same word. The many different and often deliberately ambiguous ways in which language is used in design activities can work against you. For instance, the need to move a liquid from one place to another (a function) can give rise to the use of the word 'pumping' (still a function), which immediately suggests the use of a pump (solution). This link between the words we use quickly forges a link between the problem and a very specific type of solution structure. However, there are many other possibilities for solving the problem of bringing liquid from A to B than by the use of a pump.

The 'function trees' come with their own peril. Because the design problem gets so nicely split up, people tend to think that the sub-functions each belong to a different sub-solution, to a different part in the design. But if you make a separate part for every function you produce a very inefficient design.

ANALOGIES

Designers often talk figuratively about their design, using an analogy to describe the design in an indirect way.

In a case study, there is a description of how a group of engineers, working on a long rod that had to hinge somewhere in the middle, naturally talked about an 'arm' with an 'elbow', and their subsequent design clearly showed this heritage. In this way, such figures of speech do not just help designer communicate, they can also assist creativity.

In an analogy, you use the similarity between your design problem and something else to help you describe your concept solutions, or to help you think of a novel one. It is like hitchhiking on earlier work, or on ideas from outside the direct design field. For instance, in mechanical design, analogies of Nature are often particularly fruitful. In nature, all kind of mechanical problems have been 'solved' by evolution, often in very elegant and surprising ways. There are numerous examples in popular design mythology, including the invention of Velcro and mimicking not-quite-smooth sharkskin to clad the hull of racing sailing boats.

These analogies are more than useful: it is often impossible to beat Nature if the problems you face are really similar. Nature does have its limitations, though. For instance, in Nature it is impossible to rotate anything that is alive around an axis. If that had been possible, we would undoubtedly have had wheels instead of legs...

There is a complete creativity technique based on the use of analogies, called Synectics. In Synectics, the choice of analogy is generally not free, but based on 'creative confrontation': you force an analogy between your design problem and something completely different. The stranger the fit, the greater the chance of seeing your design problem in a new light, maximizing the ability of the analogy to yield interesting results.

FRAMES

When you 'frame' a problem, you impose a view on the problem that implies a solution, or at least a direction to follow. This is often the only way to achieve a design solution, design problems can be so ill-structured and difficult that you must propose a frame (impose some kind of order) and experiment with it.

For example, a UK architectural firm was asked to design a modern, round chapel in the square courtyard of an old university college. They struggled with this for quite a while, drawing plans how to position a round thing in a square. Being modernist, they did not want to put it in the middle, but where to put it then? The whole shape of the chapel and its construction method also kept changing, which led to bitter arguments within the design team. Finally, one of the senior partners looked in on the project, and said: 'It's not a chapel, it's a boat'. That was it. The frame 'boat' redefined and specified the problem in such a way that it could easily be solved. The placing within the square was suddenly not a problem, they could moor the chapel on either side. Achieving an interesting shape and construction method also went smoothly within the 'boat' frame. Good frames have this ability to bring coherence to a design problem and direct the solution process. They are a powerful tool in the hands of a good designer.

But frames should be used with some flexibility. It is possible that even though you adopted a frame that seemed promising, you cannot reach a satisfactory solution. When you have tried everything to make the design work, but you find that it is inadequate, you will have to 'reframe'. This means taking a giant step back, to reconsider the very basis on which you have been working, to rethink your view of the problem.

This is not easy to do. These are the moments of real crisis in a design project. You are effectively pulling the rug out from under yourself. I'm afraid that reframing is part and parcel of designing. Any frame is only a provisional solution to the design problem, just a tool to help reach a solution. If it doesn't work, you have to try something else.

STRATEGIES

All designers have their own pet strategies, and some of mine are dispersed throughout this book. But there should be a warning attached to all this well-meant advice: which strategy will yield the best result depends very much on the nature and interpretation of the design problem, and the capabilities of the designer. You have to find out what suits you, and be extremely flexible in the way you work.

There is not one single best way to solve a design problem. The strategies designers adopt can be very different, almost contradictory. In a study, professional designers who were given a single very simple design assignment, employed five very different strategies. Some worked from the abstract to the concrete, starting at a level that was much more general than the assignment itself. Others more or less took the assignment for what it was and, after an analysis, they split it up into sub-problems, which they solved separately. These sub-solutions where then assembled together in the final design.

Some experienced designers, quite surprisingly, adopted a complete design solution from one of their earlier projects, and adapted this ready-made solution to the particulars of this problem situation. This led to some very surprising designs that would never have been created by only considering this simple problem.

The strategy that seemed to work the best for this particular design problem was to pose or identify priorities, solve the high-priority problems first and then adapt all the other solutions to this 'core design'.

And then there were some that just worked quite randomly, who browsed their way through the problem, jumping between sub-problems and between problem and solution without any clear strategy.

These were just the general strategies: on a more detailed level you could see designers change strategies in a split second.

DRAWING

Drawing is important in design. Not so much as a medium for making pretty pictures, but as the medium for visual and spatial thinking. You don't just draw an image that you already have in your head, you invent and construct images by drawing.

This makes sketching one of the key skills for a designer. And again, not so much the brilliant execution of complete images, but the production of ugly little sketches that help you think about your design. The kind of sketches that only you yourself will ever understand. Designers develop various kinds of drawing that have different levels of data. These range from a 'visual shorthand' when dealing with the general principle of an idea or design concept, to more elaborate sketches which are needed to figure out the form of the design, and on to complete sketches that are really meant for communication.
If you master all these sketching levels, you will command a visual language that is every bit as powerful as the spoken or written word.

The infamous 'writer's block' has its counterpart in the visual realm: the fear of blank sheets of paper. Most of us recognise this: you are all set to start sketching ideas... and nothing comes. In my own experience, just putting pen to paper and drawing a random line helps to break the spell. Just start, and your thoughts will develop. The act of drawing will clarify your thought.

However, there are many different styles of designers. Some are avid drawers, others make models or manage to design almost exclusively with words. Whatever you do, you need a medium in which you are fluent, so that you can put down your developing design ideas. If you cannot express your design, you cannot evolve your ideas.

EMERGENCE

The design tools we have been talking about are all based on getting your goals and priorities straight, by using functions or frames, and to guide your design process from there by using analogies or explicit design strategies.

However, design is more anarchic than that. In the heat of working on a design challenge it may easily happen that the set of proposed solutions suddenly develops a will of its own, suggesting the next steps to be taken, or even a complete solution. Things start to cohere and 'come together' in an almost automatic way. A solution emerges from nowhere.

This requires some openness to the possibility that a solution or idea might suddenly materialise, ready made, without anyone putting it in there. Many designers have reported this, for instance the furniture designer Geoffrey Harcourt: 'As a matter of fact, the solution that I came up with wasn't a solution to the problem at all. I never saw it as that... But when the chair was actually put together, in a way it solved the problem quite well, but from a completely different angle, a completely different point of view.' What a designer needs in this situation is some creativity in recognising the solution, a readiness to look at the design in yet another way once it is finished.

Design literature is full of stories like these – some true, some probably spurious. But it is certainly true that, for instance, many products that have been designed for the handicapped have morphed into something else and found applications in major market segments. This chaotic element of design nicely undermines much of what is said in this book, which is all aimed at solving the right problem by coming up with the right solution. That is so exciting about design – you never know.

BEING A DESIGNER

DESIGN TEAMS

SHARED UNDERSTANDING

Being a member of a design team means having to communicate with designers from other disciplines. This is a subtle process. Because of their different backgrounds, team members will never fully understand each other, and they will never completely share one view on the design. However, to work well together, they do need to share ideas and a mode of working. Moreover, you need to share the design frame (see page 132), a view on the design problem that also indicates a route toward a solution. The design frame is developed early on in the design project, and is usually revised several times. For the team to cooperate successfully it is vital that all designers understand and adopt the design frame. Otherwise, the separate design processes of the individual team members will scatter in different directions.

How do you achieve a shared frame among designers who have widely different backgrounds? Research has shown that the team member who has an idea for a design frame will introduce it to the others in a very modest, carefully worded proposal. The frame owner tends to draw in his colleagues by leaving things purposefully vague, wording the proposal as a question, and invites the others to complete his half-finished sentences. The frame idea is thereby transferred to the group in a manner that is not just an explanation of an idea, but is also a process of adoption, a transfer of ownership.

In communicating frames, designers use the vaguest statements to convince the team members to follow their general line of thought. This may seem strange, because to really have an impact, a frame needs to be as precise as possible. Yet, you may not want to fully commit to your frame proposal because you are never quite sure whether the frame will be acceptable to the others and appropriate for the design project. Communication within a design team is a subtle art all by itself.

DESIGNSPEAK

Designers in a team need to share a language to talk about the design. Because the design solution is still vague in the early stages of the project, teams tend to develop their own nicknames for certain parts or functions of the design. This impressionistic, deliberately vague vocabulary is important: using more concrete words could 'freeze' the image of what the design could be, much too soon.

Language is an important tool in design, but should be used carefully. The meaning of many words which refer to the design can actually change dramatically during the course of a design project. Their meaning should develop from the vague and general to the ever more detailed, but is not uncommon that a certain word will take on a completely different meaning in the heat of design concept development. These nicknames or 'private words' are often based on the shared experience of earlier projects or products, which are referred to in shorthand. As a result, a design team that wrestles with a complicated conceptual phase can develop a real subculture which is notoriously incomprehensible to the outside world, and to new team members as well. If you join a design team later on in a project, it takes a while to figure out what they are talking about.

The use of this vague, personalised 'designspeak' does have its drawbacks – things often go wrong because of the impressionistic use of certain words. Designers often think they understand each other, while substantial differences in interpretation lurk under the surface. These differences always emerge in the end, because a completed design is concrete and very unambiguous, and requires all differences in interpretation to be ironed out. Unfortunately, this can come painfully late in the design project.

SIGN LANGUAGE

Design teams do not, of course, just use words to communicate. They use drawings, gestures and body language as well. This has caused problems for the development of Collaborative Design Systems. These computer systems support the communication of designers at different locations so that they can work together as a team.

Recently co-designing has become more and more important, since production is often done in countries with lower wages, while the design itself is still being made in the richer countries, closer to the markets. This means that design information has started to travel digitally across the world. Impressive computer systems have been developed which allow multiple designers to work on a drawing simultaneously – to gesture and point things out to one another with hands that are virtually suspended over a work surface.

These computer systems have become the ultimate design playthings, with cameras and fast connections which give the impression of really being present at the other location. However, recent research has shown – counterintuitively – that the narrower channels of communication actually result in better design work, because the designers are forced to be as specific as possible, and to cut down on the vaguer forms of designspeak.

Even with these systems, though, the conventional wisdom still applies that distributed design teams need to be physically brought together at least once, to get to know each other, in order to cooperate successfully. If they know each other they will be better equipped to pick up the weaker signals that are so important in design communication, like the hesitation before an answer. This is particularly important in the case of cross-cultural design. It is impossible to design together if you are not acquainted with each other's cultures. The best way to give and receive criticism is very different in East and West.

TEAM ROLES

Design education has traditionally focussed on training individuals. But these same individuals will have to cooperate in design teams once they finish their studies. There is an obvious need to develop cooperative working skills, and a deeper question about the profile of the designers that are currently being educated. For teamwork you need design specialists who have a profound knowledge of one aspect of the design field. What you do not need are broadly educated 'universal' designers. A team of generalists will just get into each other's way. In team situations, you also need a special brand of designer that can act as project leaders.

A project leader has many roles to play in a design project. For one, he has to coordinate the planning and division of the tasks. That is not easy because design tasks are manifold and very different in nature and length. What often happens is that the designers with the shortest task will start bothering the others with their results. As a consequence, the designers with the longest (and often hardest) task will be the ones that are most often interrupted. It is also difficult to figure out beforehand which tasks will need the results of others to get under way, and what will be the longest chain of these dependencies. This 'critical path' ultimately determines the length of the design project.

Tasks are often assigned to team members in coherent roles, which they will perform for the duration of the project. For example, one person will be the 'information handler', another will guard the design's essential requirements, a third collects ideas. We know that in the heat of any design project, all of these tasks will run together, with concept ideas typically causing the requirements to be refined or modified, which in turn creates a need for more information. But as long as it is clear who does what, these discussions will remain clear and efficient.

What you want to avoid in design team work is a situation in which several designers are actually doing the same task, together, and keep disagreeing with each other's moves at every step. Then design teams can be much slower than just working alone.

DIVERGENT PAIRS

Working in a design team can be a rough ride, with a lot of potential for serious conflict along the way. On the other hand, being part of a really good design team is a fantastic experience.

There has been a lot of discussion about the question how to put together a good design team. One theory is that you should make a team of designers as diverse as possible. Put a hard-boiled technologist together with a pure shape designer and their natural talents will blend into something sublime. A sort of amalgamate designer, whose qualities are more than the sum of the two parts. It could work that way, but this could also be a recipe for disaster. If you couple designers in divergent pairs you assume that they are good communicators, honest, inspiring and modest, each being completely receptive to the other's world. In other words, these designers should be saints. Something tells me that this would be very unusual.

Design team selection is an important issue, of which we understand very little. It is just so complicated that we not have an overview of the many variables needed to be OK for a design team to thrive. This is one of the many areas in design where we are still learning the lessons through trial and error in practice. For instance, some recent cases have suggested that it would be preferable for all team members to have skills within their own design fields that are at a similar level of expertise, so that no designer will be completely dominant and people can work as equals.

THE WINNING TEAM

Winning teams are surprisingly brittle. You can't manufacture a winning team, the only thing you can do is make sure that the circumstances are conducive. You put together designers with the right training, background and mix of characters, and can only hope that an atmosphere develops in which you will get the best out of everyone. But you never know when the design project will really start to flow.

For a research project, I observed a team of designers from one of the leading US product design agencies. They were experienced designers, and they had been working together for a couple of years.
The moment they got the design assignment they split up the tasks: 'Mr. Schedule' did the planning and project management, one dealt with information management, a third was appointed Head Designer. They interpreted the assignment together, then fluently worked their way though the information, listing the requirements on a whiteboard. However, the idea phase was strangely chaotic. They seemed to get stuck. They had lots of ideas about the complete product and some partial construction details, but without a clear dominant concept or central theme. To the onlooker they gave the impression that they were running out of time, but they didn't seem to mind. About ten minutes before the deadline, Mr. Schedule intervened, saying something like 'Let's wrap this up'. While simultaneously working on one big sheet of paper, the team made a drawing of a design concept in which all problems were solved. Apparently, the solution had been there between them all the time, but they had not even needed to communicate it explicitly. They knew what they were doing. Fluent and masterful.

It was like those clips on television of a building that is dynamited - but then played backwards. Everything coming together miraculously. Now *that's* teamwork.

AROUND DESIGN

DESIGNING IN CONTEXT

THE FORCEFIELD AROUND DESIGN

We have talked about design as if it were an isolated activity, but of course it never is. The purpose of design is to develop something for the wider world, and that wider world is intimately woven into any design project. Design not only takes place in a context, it is permeated by it.

The design project is always shaped by the general needs and concrete users of the design-to-be. The designer has some autonomy during the conceptual stage of the design project, but for most of the time the designer will have to contend with an indefinite number of stakeholders. In the end, the designer has to produce a design that can be defended before the stakeholders because they have the final say.

This aspect of design work is almost unknown to design students, who develop their knowledge and core skills in the sheltered environment of a design school. The 'realistic' design assignments they are presented with during their education are never quite realistic in this sense. After graduation they are suddenly pushed out of this playground into the cold wide world. Of course, they never realise that they have been working in a playground until it is too late. They are then confronted with the difficulties of making a living in a world which they do not really understand. There is a feeling of powerlessness involved, since all the design knowledge they have acquired in school has not prepared them for the kind of problems they encounter now. These problems all concern how to manage the context around design.

This can be a very hard transition, which usually occurs at a sensitive time in the development of the designer as a person. Some adapt quite easily, others have much more difficulty and a few just don't survive. They get pushed around, become disoriented and can personally get hurt in this confrontation. It's not necessarily the worst designers that fail in their first job.

DESIGN AS A NECESSARY EVIL

There is a common misconception among design students that the world will welcome them, because everybody appreciates creativity and the novelty of design. Unfortunately, this isn't so. Many companies tend to see designers as a necessary evil, and treat them accordingly. Of course, companies know they need to innovate to be competitive. And for innovation they must deal with these strange-looking 'creatives' called designers. But they do not really have to like it.

For a company, innovation is something of a two-edged sword: it is nice to think creatively about the future, everybody likes brainstorming, but really changing the communication, marketing, products or production processes in a company is quite another thing. Real change involves letting go of set structures and cherished habits. While beginning something new, the old is inadvertently killed and buried. It is important to be aware that often, change involves a kind of mourning process. It actually helps to use the mourning process as a metaphor, since one can recognise the same stages of shock, denial, anger and resignation.

With a real innovation you can touch the very foundation and identity of a company. This can result in a huge and irrational resistance to the designer. Often, it is necessary to endlessly keep explaining the benefits of the innovation in order to persuade people to accept the new design. This is a slow process, but people must get used to the idea on an emotive level before they can really embrace the innovation. In the worst case, there could be some kind of organised resistance to change, which can be very effective because organisations are, by their very nature, built to perpetuate a stable situation. The wrath of an organisation scorned can be terrible.

As a designer the best you can hope for is to encounter some mixed feelings, but even outright hatred is not outside the range of possible emotions you might innocently evoke. You are not always the bringer of good news.

CROSS PURPOSES

Designers do not have quite the same goals as the people they work for. A designer is a creative person who continually seeks new challenges to stimulate his/her own creative development. Designers selfishly use a client's project for this purpose.

Designers bring their own criteria, their own quality standards, to a project. This introduces an extra tension to the relationship between a designer and their client/employer. There is a very real potential for conflict.

Often the differences between designer and client are easily glossed over in the early, vague stages of a design project. Those early stages are happily creative, where both parties enjoy playing with ideas without making any serious commitments of time or money. But this changes dramatically when the design becomes concrete. At this stage, the real underlying differences in opinion suddenly come to the surface, and the very nature of the designer/client relationship could be changed beyond recognition. This is a potentially dangerous phase, where a new working relationship must be developed quickly.

As a designer you are always the weaker partner in these discussions, so conflict is not in your interest. If you want to get your way, you must be the diplomat. In a project, you should try to avoid unpleasant surprises, such as sudden yes-or-no situations. Most communication between designer and the employer/client is a slow process of tuning in on each other, with the designer typically trying to soften criteria which he thinks could hinder an innovative solution. The designer has to ensure that there is enough common ground with both party's design criteria, otherwise agreement will never be reached. Some designers are extremely good at this. Their designs are social and diplomatic works of art.

NATURAL ENEMIES

Innovation almost always breeds resistance to change. A designers' role embodies this innovation – a role that can easily clash with the interests of some of the company's (other) employees. These self-interests are often embodied by people in certain roles in the company. They are the natural enemies which a designer must contend with.

In product design, the plant manager (head of production) has such a role. When you approach him, the plant manager will typically start to explain that he has just, after many years of hard work, managed to put together an efficient and smooth running factory. And here you are, the designer, bringing drawings of a product that will upset everything... From his perspective, some reservations are quite understandable. This resistance can run very very deep: I once worked for a company where a product development project couldn't be finalised because the plant managers refused to make a prototype. It turned out that the salary and bonuses of these plant managers depended on making the current production as efficient as possible. Quantity was everything. It was clearly not in their interest to halt the machines to help product development make a few prototypes. In these circumstances, everybody has their own version of the truth. They were as right as we were. But someone had made the mistake of organising the company in such a way that only short term efficiency would be rewarded. Companies that are listed on the stock exchange, and have to deliver glowing figures to their shareholders every three months, are quite notorious for such myopic behaviour. As a designer, they are very hard to work for. Design is always a long term investment.

There is also the age-old feud between the Marketing and Design departments: The Battle for the User. Within an innovation project, both the marketing department and the designers have their own opinions about the preferences of the user. Marketing sees them more as buyers, which is crucial because they have to give a verdict on the design when the management asks them whether the product will sell or not. The design department, on the other hand, thinks it knows all about the real needs of the user, as a person using and enjoying the design. Clashes are common. Yet great things will only happen if they work together.

RISK

Companies take a considerable risk by developing something new. In product design, the failure rates are very high. There is an infamous 10% figure hanging over product design – some research long ago showed that only 10% of product concepts are successful on the market. So, 90% never make it to the market or they get there and flop.

So companies tend to seek safety in every possible way. There can be protection (or at least reassurance) in market research, or in the predictions of trend analysts. There is also some security in getting a big name designer to create a product for you, since their status and the publicity they generate can help the product become a success.

Alas, there is also safety in big markets, as well as in neutral design. This means that complicated consumer products which require a great investment to develop, like computers and printers, are still predominantly grey boxes. Their designs are not offensive, but there is also nothing to enjoy. It is a pity that the products we use most intensively, for so many hours a day, never seem to evolve beyond utter drabness. It would take a very good designer with a lot of courage and patience to convince companies to stick their neck out.

A student of mine once got involved in the development of an electronic toy for girls. Unimaginatively, the company had decided on a rounded, flowery shape and the colour was, yes, bright pink. Apparently they weren't sure that enough girls would want it, because a later prototype was grey, to 'also appeal to boys'. A grey flower, just what the boy in me always wanted. This is one of the 90% of products that – in this case deservedly – never made it to the market.

SKINNY PROJECTS

Because design projects are risky, a company is definitely not going to invest too much money in them. Most design projects are skinny, up to the point of almost starving to death.

This is related to the way the contracts and planning for design projects are put together by both parties. Normally, a general phase model of design is used to list all the activities that must take place and an estimation is made of how much time they will take. A complete price for the project (phase) is then calculated by multiplying the total number of hours with the hourly rate of the designer.

The problem is this – we know that design is inherently an iterative learning process, and these linear planning models never take that into account. The calculations are actually a kind of best case scenario, in which all the design activities run smoothly and efficiently. We know that this never happens. More importantly, the learning process, which has been kept out of the time equation, is actually what makes design so interesting and it is the thing that really determines the design quality.

As it is, any slight delay or unexpected twist in the project immediately leads to problems which have to be solved during non-billable hours.

It is not impossible to plan a project that takes the iterative, learning side of design into account. At the start of a project you can usually see at which point there will be iterations, because they are always associated with novelty. It is also quite easy to estimate the number of iterations, based on your experience ('well, this is a new production technique for us, and last time it took us two design concepts before we really got it right, remember?'). Just estimate the iterations, and plan for them. Never pretend design is a linear activity.

ISO 9000 AND THE HOLY PROCESS

Traditionally, products that came off the production line were tested before they went onto the market. But taking samples and torturing them to breaking point is costly and wasteful. So quality testing has moved to the testing of a prototype and making a very precise description of production procedures. If we know that the thing can work in principle, then if they are made carefully all the copies will do so too. So quality assurance has moved from end-of-line towards the prototype and the production process itself.

More recently, this line of reasoning has been led all the way back to the design process. The idea is that a well designed product will be of good quality. A logical step to take, which nobody could argue with. So industrious standards institutes set out to develop standards for the design process, resulting in the ISO 9000 series of standards. The idea is that if you carefully go through the phases that are laid out in the ISO 9000 texts, and produce documents to prove that you followed those steps, then your design will be of good quality.

This is highly questionable. The standards institutes have taken certain generally useful and accepted phase models as the basis for this text. However, we all know how widely design processes can differ, and that the phase models, though generally accepted, represent just one view of designing.

But the most fundamental problem is this: does a well-run design process really assure a good design?

PART OF A LARGER WHOLE

General circumstances that are normally the backdrop to a design stage can suddenly jump in and upset any design project at any time. These include things like shifts in the market, where trends are set and overtaken by others, or the ups and downs of macroeconomic fortunes.
Design projects can be complicated and slow, and sizeable projects usually have to survive economic cycles and management changes. There are two possible responses to this: either try to do them more quickly, or to make the design project very robust.

An extreme case of the latter is the designing and building of a technically, socially and politically complex object like a modern art museum. Such a project could take up to twenty years, so the design firm has to ensure a good project layout and documentation, since it is quite certain that the people who participate in the project will change during the years. No one who was there at the beginning will still be working on the project when it finally finishes. This goes for the design team as well as for the client side. Such long term projects have a whole new set of problems to contend with. Every design idea and design decision must be made explicit and written down, because there will be a continuous stream of newcomers to the project who have to know what has happened. Implicit choices have to be avoided because they can be more easily called into question by the newcomers, and the whole project might become a circular mess.

Speeding up a design project is the other way to avoid interruptions, and has the additional advantage of lowering the risk of being out-of-date by the time you enter the market. For instance, in the automobile industry, huge efforts were made to reorganise the design process to reduce the development time of a car from about four years in the 1980s to about two years today. And there is pressure to be even faster than that.

DESIGNING THE FUTURE OF A COMPANY

Companies take pains to develop statements about what they are, and what they want to be. These policy statements are often general, vague and not very informative. Every company wants to 'produce maximum value for the customer' with a 'dedicated workforce'. Still, this gives some general idea of direction, and it can be interesting to realise what is not included. These policy statements are the starting point for more concrete strategies which work towards attaining those goals.

In this way, running a business and doing design work are quite similar. Both are processes where analytical capability and creativity are used together to develop plans for the future. This similarity often results in an intuitive rapport between managers and designers, a recognition that comes from struggling with the same kind of problems.

The trouble is that these design-like problems of policy and strategy formulation are not tackled in a design-like way. In design, it is unwise to set goals without exploring what is feasible. You have to explore the possibilities first, by developing and evaluating sketchy solutions. You alternate between the problem and possible solutions, developing them together. In management, the classic internal and external analyses (Strengths Weaknesses Opportunities Threats) used to develop the policy and strategies of a company are purely problem focussed.

This is where designers could play a new role, mapping the results of ambitions and strategies by creatively exploring their results through thought experiments or pilot projects.

AROUND DESIGN

MANAGING
DESIGN

INNOVATION MANAGEMENT

The innovation process has many steps, from the development of a new company policy and strategy, to the consideration of the product portfolio, down to the nuts and bolts of the design process and the introduction of the design to the market. This process is often mapped as a linear scheme with boxes and arrows, like an extended version of a design process.

The difficulty in these larger innovation processes is that, in contrast to design processes, which tend to take place within a design department or design agency, the different stages of the innovation process are done by different people at different levels in the company hierarchy. And the roles of the departments relative to one another are not fixed: they need to change dramatically in the course of the innovation project. Marketing, for instance, should move from an initial qualitative analysis of opportunities and threats to the creative role of exploring new markets. This prompts another analysis to set the product-market criteria, which moves into developing a marketing plan for the product. And in between are a number of design-driven phases where marketing is in a vague consulting role (and should, by the way, not keep shooting down concepts by constantly saying 'this will not sell').

The design role changes from the initial support of the policy making process (providing concrete ideas that help visualise the different policy options), to providing general design concepts as input for exploratory market research. Once that is done design takes the lead in developing the definitive design concepts, which have to be tested and embodied in close cooperation with the marketing and production people.

Needless to say, these different roles that require such various amounts of engagement and responsibility are difficult to play in one and the same project. The one time you are a creative visualiser, the other time a consultant, then the lead party responsible for the core of the project. Making a mistake in the role you play, for instance pushing a favourite design concept while the market is still being explored, can be counterproductive.

DESIGN MANAGEMENT

A company needs to express itself in a coordinated way. This used to be modestly called house-style management, which involved things like the style of business cards and printed letterheads. House-style management would typically include the production of big fat house-style manuals full of rules to be zealously policed.

But lately companies have realised that a strongly expressed identity may grow to be a 'brand', and be seen as an almost human entity by the market. Brands can be a very effective platform for market communication, and are considered valuable money-earners in their own right.

But how do you make a brand? Building a clear picture of a company is something of a holistic enterprise, which involves many departments: Management, Marketing, Publicity, Graphic Design, Product Design and possibly Service Development. To get all of them to express a coherent message requires a lot of coordination. This difficult task has given rise to a comparatively new discipline: Design Management.

Design Managers operate between all the above departments, shuttle-wise. They guard the expressed identity of the company and develop its brands by steering the work in the departments. They try to be the glue that holds together the companies' self expression.

They exert a far-reaching influence on the 'creative departments' of a company, based on the importance of company identity and branding. The 'creative departments', including the design department, don't always like that. Their reflex is to always struggle to maximize their design freedom. But there are advantages to having a strong design management too. As a designer, you may notice that companies with good design management are much easier to work for efficiently. They do not need to use your design concepts to discover what they really want.

FORGOTTEN STEPS

Considering how much time and effort (including hugely expensive consultancy hours) is spent on the formulation of company policy and strategy, it is surprising to see how little effort is made to translate these general policy statements into concrete design briefs in a valid way. People become enchanted with policy statements and forget to translate them into reality.

Design briefs tend to be based on some general idea that has emerged from nowhere, accompanied by a statement that this product-to-be will help attain company goals. Clearly, there is a step missing here.
To really make a well-considered connection between policy and design, you need to enter a kind of pre-design process, a creative analysis of possible design directions and preliminary (qualitative) market research. The goal of this process is to determine what general features the product should possess to reach its market goals, and to further the ambitions of the company.

You have to creatively translate the company policy into a design brief. This can be done without first designing the product. The translation process results in rather vague product descriptions, like we need a 'something' with these and these properties. This is a blurry statement, containing some basic ideas and general specifications, which should leave plenty of room for the designer. Still, designers do not always appreciate this. They see it as part of their job to question all the assumptions behind a design brief, and try to squeeze out as much freedom as they can.

But there are many advantages to designers if the translation has already been made. A well-executed translation of policy into design brief can give confidence that the designer is working on the right product. Right for the market, and right for the company. There are few more thankless jobs in this world than that of a designer working on a design that is based on an ill-conceived design brief. The product will inevitably fail, or fail to live up to expectations. And in the end the designer, as the most visible contributor to the product, will be blamed for its failure.

SKUNKWORKS

As a designer, you are involved with just one of the processes that will lead to a new activity of the company. There are other things that need to be developed in parallel: the organisation of the company might have to be changed, the market has to be scanned and addressed in novel ways, the production and distribution has to be adapted, sometimes overhauled completely. There are many vital connections between these changes in product, market, organisation and production, and overlooking one of these links can put the whole innovation in jeopardy.

People have tried to control the innovation process by first developing it at a kind of test site, outside the main organisation. The official term is 'skunkworks'. By using such a breeding ground, you can at least avoid having the development problems and implementation problems all at the same time. This special innovative cell can also be used to train the people who will implement the change within the 'real' organisation. This works reasonably well, although the breeding grounds tend to become much too innovative, and drift too far away from the main company to be of any real influence. Skunkworks then become little satellite companies all by themselves. They are fun, though. The ultimate playgrounds for designers.

CHANGE AGENTS

What makes innovation so hard is that formal organisations tend to be stiff and quite resistant to change. Any innovation process is new (by definition) and quite different than what people are used to. Most people resist change, but in all departments and walks of life there are often people who really like it. The success or failure of an innovation depends on these few flexible and creative people within an organisation. This is an informal role, but it is vital. You need just a few of these so-called 'change agents', sprinkled through the organisation.

These people are not easy to spot because they can have all kinds of different formal positions, but within their own group, they are the ones who will undertake new challenges and help the others move forward. They also tend to take care of aspects that go beyond their own responsibility. They often know, and work with, the innovative people in other parts of the company, and manage to get things done on the basis of these personal contacts. Any innovation process relies on these informal inbetweeners who ensure the fluidity of an organisation.

As a designer, co-responsible for an innovation, you should get to know them as quickly as possible, interest them in your project, and work with them. They are vital allies.

THE DESIGN FORTRESS

Design departments are like little fortresses. Secrecy is ostensibly to avoid having their ideas stolen by 'the competition'. But I often get the impression that it has more to do with protecting designers from people in their own company.

Designers tend to isolate themselves because they hope that will give them the freedom to explore and experiment in ways that may not always be understood by the company. Design is an odd creative process, which involves a creative playfulness that is uncommon in most other company departments.

This peculiar nature of design can lead to grave misunderstandings. For instance, an intermediate but unsatisfactory design concept can be seen as a failure, while it may just be an experiment which is part of a normal design exploration.

An interesting story is the development of a new Dutch passport, some years ago. It turned out to be difficult to find a plastic layer that would seal the photo page, withstand heat, moisture, vandalism and that would not be easy to forge. The designers experimented with different plastic layers and had them tested in a lab. At one point, these test results were leaked to the press, which led to headlines like 'The Failure of The New Passport'. Questions were asked in parliament about the squandering of public money, etc. This caused the designers to loose the freedom to experiment further. They had to settle for the best alternative among those already tested, which was not ideal. The end of the freedom to experiment is the end of the design process. That is why design is such a secretive activity.

BUILDING TRUST

In a company, design and innovation are often surrounded by uncertainty and suspicion. An innovative design project is expensive, and you never know whether a design project will yield a good result. There is no guaranteed success. In the early stages of a project, the company has little else to go on than their faith in the designers they hired.

Such a relationship of trust between company and designer cannot be built in one day. That is why, as a designer, you often need to talk with a client several times before you are asked to do even a small project. If that goes well, they trust you a bit more, and you might be eligible for the challenging, bigger projects.

Building a relationship with a company and maintaining their trust in you is a vital skill for designers. Trust is a vulnerable, personal feeling. Once a relationship of trust is ruined, it can seldom be restored. People feel personally betrayed and hurt if this happens. On the other hand, if you manage to fulfil the trust put upon you, they easily turn to you again the next time they need a design. A relationship of trust is a long term commitment.

This trust-building strategy of trying a small project first is quite common, but there are other ways in which you further their trust in you, as a designer. You can try to convince the company that your design project will yield results by presenting solid-looking phased project plans with lots of Go-NoGo decisions. This convinces the company that they have some measure of control over the project. Many of the so-called 'progress meetings' you have during a design project serve no other apparent function than to reassure the company that you still know what you are doing.

Everything runs on trust.

THE WALL OF SECRECY

I personally believe that in the end the wall of secrecy which designers erect around themselves does not help them, that it leads to the absurdity of closed project offers based on a linear plan for a process that is so uncertain. But most designers don't see this as a problem anymore: they have resigned themselves to the 'fact' that you always run out of time before a deadline, and that you will have to work late into the night to achieve the quality you want, out of your own time. I hold that this need not be so, that we should not accept the results of our own misconceptions as 'facts of life'.

There are design firms that have taken a different route, and have decided to become completely transparent to their clients. They do not give the client a closed project offer, but provide weekly reports which specify the work they did (accompanied by a bill and an estimation of the amount of work still to be done). This weekly report means that the design project is completely transparent: it is quite impossible to keep things secret or sweep them under the carpet. If part of the project turns out to be harder than had been expected, this is reported to the client, and extra time is asked to deal with the problem. After all, both designer and client have one common objective: that enough time is spent on the design so that it can be done well. This relieves the designers of unnecessary deadline stress, since they know they will have enough time to achieve a good design.

SIZE MATTERS

Design departments are hard to manage because nothing is constant. They run from project to project, so everything keeps starting up and ending. There is very little natural stability. You tend to get into unpleasant cycles: at times you can be extremely busy, but if you get too many projects, this limits your time to acquire new work for the future – so these busy periods will alternate with quieter ones. Sometimes, disconcertingly quiet.

It doesn't help that design firms and design departments tend to strive for bigger and bigger projects, because they are often more interesting. This always means biting off a little more than you know that you can comfortably chew.

But there is something like an 'ideal size' for a design company which depends on the size of projects that it takes on. Portfolio management is everything in such a project based company. A rule of thumb says that you should be large enough to do 2 of your biggest projects in parallel, and still have about a quarter of your staff working on smaller projects. This is a good mix of big and small, so that you don't become overly dependent on big projects, and can easily reassign your workforce to smaller projects when a big one finishes. Smaller projects allow you to reach a comfortable balance.

There is a danger in doing too many small projects, though: you can easily get swamped by them as well. I once advised a design department where every designer reported working on 20 projects. It turned out that these projects only existed in progress meetings where everybody kept looking around expectantly, hoping the other might have had time to do something since the last meeting... All progress meetings, but no progress. The solution to this is simple, of course: as a designer you should avoid working on more than 2 or 3 projects at a time. Working on projects intensely means you'll finish them a lot quicker. The only difficulty is to convince the managers that postponing work on a project for a couple of weeks, but completing it quickly, is much more efficient than starting halfheartedly and letting it drag on forever. Management often likes to promise immediate action to clients, and that is how you ruin a design organisation.

MAJOR DESIGN PROJECTS

Smaller design projects can be relatively easy to organise, when it is still possible for a single person to get a complete overview of what needs to be done in all stages of the project. The organisation is composed by taking the central process of design, and seeing what resources are needed at every step.

But in major design projects, this kind of comprehensive overview inevitably gets lost. Then, you have several design teams working on different components or aspects of the problem and solution, with many specialists involved. This is a huge coordination nightmare.

The bigger design projects tend be organised into teams who work on parts of the solution. The interfaces between these components of the design become the issues that need to be discussed between the design teams. So in big projects, the diagrams of the product and the organisation look similar. But that is not all. The critical issues of scarcity and resource allocation concern everyone, and they need to be centrally coordinated. This is not only for the 'universal' resources of time (planning) and money (budget). Depending on the design, there are other common resources that need to be managed. In car design for instance, there is a weight manager. Every part of the product gets a weight allowance, that the designers have to stay within. If they get too heavy, negotiations determine where weight can be saved. There also is a space manager, who has to make sure that the designed parts stay within the three dimensional area assigned to them. You can only use space once.

All the minor coordination problems that we encounter in smaller design projects become explicit organisational issues in such a major project.

THERAPY

When a design department or design agency does not run smoothly, everybody has an opinion about what should be done to improve things. Designers are know-it-alls. But these different opinions are mostly based upon quite different impressions of what the actual situation is, and how it came about. When trying to improve the state of affairs, it is important to do a little investigation that helps the designers to move away from these conflicting opinions and opposing positions towards the level of the concrete design experiences they all share.

One way to do this is to ask each designer to write down 10 positive and 10 negative experiences they had during their projects. And then, as a group, have the designers combine their experiences in a list and rank them in importance. They are then asked to link these concrete design experiences to possible causes (there are standard categories for this, such as: was it the way the project was managed? was it the process? did it have to do with a type of client?). It always amazes me how much agreement suddenly emerges. The neutral overview, built on their own concrete design experiences, helps to generate consensus on what needs to be done. These sessions have a therapeutic value all by themselves.

It is a pity that things have to get out of control before designers start taking their own organisation and way of working seriously.

THE LIFE CYCLE OF THE DESIGNER

Designers seem to be extraordinarily short-lived. There are not that many people who are still active designers, ten years after graduating. How can that be? What seems to happen is that designers and design agencies get completely obsessed with the short-term problems of the project at hand and that they misjudge the amount of personal maintenance it takes to stay in the design field. Consequently, they just get on with it, working ridiculously hard for about 10 years in this very challenging and creative profession, and enjoying every minute of it.

Then something snaps. How come?

One scenario is that you have allowed your inspiration to run dry. To maintain creativity you need to make sure that inspiration keeps flowing in, but designers seem to forget this in the hectic of their daily work. They basically work themselves to the bone in the production of designs. That can be fulfilling, since it is fun to work in a profession with a level of mastery, mining your considerable experience. But after a while you are only dealing with design challenges that you have seen before, and your heart just isn't in it anymore. It becomes work. What you need to do then, of course, is take a break and define new challenges for yourself that will sharpen your edge again. However, that is hard to achieve. What designers tend to do instead is to move into management-type functions, or mine their considerable qualities and experience in a different way by going into consultancy.

Another scenario is that you allowed your knowledge and skills to gradually run out of date. After all, design always pushes the boundary of what is new, and if you don't keep on learning but rely too much on old knowledge you are bound to become irrelevant in 5 to 10 years time. Your work will dry up. Time to look for a different career.

There is an urgent need to find ways of extending the life-cycle of the designer. It is quite disastrous that the people with the most experience keep dropping out of the profession so early in their career (It is also a scary thought most of the designs we see around us are made by comparative beginners!). The message should be that life-long learning is a vital part of being a designer. Invest in yourself.

POST PROJECT DEPRESSION

Design projects are quite an experience. Often they involve a great creative challenge, high stakes for all involved and project dynamics that are really unpredictable. This puts an enormous pressure on the designer. These are the kinds of situations that can bring out the best in you. Intense emotions of hope, fear, enthusiasm and uncertainty follow each other in quick succession. A roller-coaster ride.

This requires huge personal involvement by the designer. The intensity can be such that the design project becomes an absorbing world in itself, leaving the designer lost to the rest of the world. Relationships get stale, houses run down, gardens become wildernesses: the project is the only thing that counts.

Surely, the successful ending of such a project would be a cause for celebration. But somehow designers find it difficult to do this. They tend to dive into the next project. There is no time to look back, we need to move on – the grass in the future is always greener. Many design projects do not even have a clear ending. There are always a couple of things that need some follow-up so projects tend to peter out, ending in silence, in nothingness.

Psychologically speaking, this is not good for us at all. A project is a world that you have inhabited for weeks or months, maybe even years. And now that world is gone. It can leave an uncanny hollow feeling, a real psychological and physical hangover.
All the attention, commitment and momentum that kept you going through the hard times evaporate. The goals that were all-important a couple of weeks ago are now irrelevant. This sudden shock of relativity makes you feel a fool, desperately asking yourself 'Why did I let myself be dragged into it again?' Dejection can easily lead to a full-blown post-project depression: feelings of loss, emptiness, and vague discontent accompanied by a monumental dip in energy levels. It will take a while before you are back on your feet. If we want to avoid this, we really should learn to celebrate our successes.

AROUND DESIGN

DESIGN
MORALITY

CREATING VALUE AT THE COST OF VALUE

Our lives are determined by conservation laws, like the first law of thermodynamics. These laws state that whatever you do, it also costs something. You can slide down a hill, enjoying the transformation of potential energy into kinetic energy, but you have to climb up the hill again to gather new potential energy for the next slide.

This is certainly true for the physical domain, and is a good metaphor for what often happens in the human domain. One could propose a 'law of the conservation of misery'. Everything you do, no matter how good, inevitably has unwanted side effects. Designs you make to serve some people will also pollute the world, and make life harder for others.

You create value at the cost of value.

But in the human domain, this law is not a 1 : 1 matter. In design, the trick is to produce much more value than you destroy. Design is essentially the creation of value. Thinking about the positive aspects of a design should always be balanced by keeping track of the value you eliminate. As a designer, you are responsible for decisions that will affect this balance. Meaning well is just not good enough – the positive ends you have in mind for your design do not justify all means.

It is comparatively easy to avoid harming the basic human rights of people. However, often the weighing of pros and cons is not so clear. It is often a group that is not represented as a concrete stakeholder in the design project, like society or the environment, that pays the price for the value that is created for the user.

ETHICS AND DESIGN

I once worked as a junior designer on a product that claimed to be a substantial improvement in safety. And to be honest, it was. But it was uncomfortable to notice that during the design project, as during any project, compromises were struck to keep the price down. Compromises that severely influenced the durability and performance of the product. Safety was claimed, and delivered, but not more than was necessary to stay just within the limits of the law.

Laws and product standards are becoming ever more detailed to keep companies and designers from delivering dangerous products to consumers. Instruction manuals have become longer and longer, listing all the things one should not do while using a product, including some pretty amazing things that you never would have thought of. 'Do not dry your pet in the microwave' is a classic example.

The key is, of course, to act responsibly, irrespective of the standards. Unfortunately, acting responsibly is not as simple as it sounds. There are several quite disparate moral adages that can be used to determine what is ethically sound. The principles that express the duty of one person toward another, like 'do unto others as you would want them to do to you' and 'do not use other people as objects, but respect their humanity', are often incompatible with the utilitarian principles of wanting to create 'the greatest good for the greatest number of people', and the 'ends justify the means'.

These moral conflicts can be dramatic. A group of my students were so zealous in developing a home care system for the demented elderly, that they filled the home with video camera's, broadcasting the movements of the poor subject over the web to a wide array of caregivers. And the students meant well. The end of privacy and human dignity is near when people so badly want to help you.

LITTLE WHITE LIES

Apart from the grand ethics of Golden Rules and utilitarian principles of human behaviour, there is also a hidden, everyday ethics. This is about those little irregularities that can occur during a design project. Most designers will recognise the situation: you are working on a design, and it turns out to be trickier than you thought. The deadline is approaching, so you either have to cancel the meeting or present a design that is not quite hammered out. Some nice drawings and your good presentation skills will probably get you through the meeting.

The problem is that if you go through with the meeting you might end up with decisions in your design that you are not quite sure about, and that might be wrong. Reversing those decisions later on in the project will lead to a loss of face, so you could be stuck with them. In a design agency, I once spent a couple of weeks changing the very working principle of a product in a way that the client wouldn't notice. The cost of all the extra design hours alone should have been enough reason to call the client and admit the earlier mistake. But the account manager said that this was the only way to save our 'credibility'.

This is very dangerous ground. The most infamous cases of failed designs are not the result of big mistakes, but of those little decisions that make a project spin out of control. The story of the faulty design of the O-rings in the booster-rockets of the space shuttle Challenger does not contain any real villains – it doesn't even contain bad designers. The only thing that set them on the road to disaster was a supplier who preferred to say that a low temperature launch was no problem, although he didn't know for sure. He was hiding the uncertainty, trying to save face.

In the early phases of a design project many decisions are made on the basis of minimal information. You can only really understand their consequences much later in the project. If those choices are seen as decisions, instead of as proposals, they can easily lead to design disaster. Designers can't afford the luxury of having a face to save.

RISKS AND DISASTERS

Designers and engineers have been known to make some really spectacular mistakes. Products are unsafe, bridges collapse. Historians of technology have noticed that these mistakes tend to come in cycles. In an effort to make hanging bridges as lean as possible, people have overlooked particularly dangerous combinations of wind and rain. Every thirty or forty years, a bridge will be made too slim, and start dancing in the wind.

These disasters are where the whole question of designer's responsibility takes on a grim face. Designing always involves a measure of uncertainty and estimation, there is no way to completely avoid risk.
In the famous case of the Citicorp building in New York, the owner of the design firm found out that the building, with its odd frame, had not been calculated correctly. That is, the shape of the frame did not comply with all the assumptions of the calculation methods that were used. It was an unsafe structure, despite having used the normal safety factors. A once-in-twenty-years storm coming from the wrong direction could blow it over. The structure of the building was adapted quickly to keep this from ever happening. The fact that the design firm had honestly owned up to making a mistake, and set about correcting it immediately, actually led to the insurance company lowering their liability rates: the firm had demonstrated that they could act responsibly.

Different professional organisations have recognised these problems of moral responsibility and accountability, and have developed a 'professional code' for their members. These guidelines do give some basis for reflection on the moral dilemmas of everyday design practice, but they are rarely specific enough to be applied directly. They must be supplemented by a personal sense of responsibility.

I JUST WORK HERE

A designer is responsible for the things that he designs. However, this is not as straightforward and simple as it sounds. When we look at design practice, we see that in the case of the development of a morally objectionable product, or a serious accident that can be traced back to a design fault, designers often use excuses to evade to their responsibility.

The top ten amoral excuses:
'I was just a small cog on the wheel...'
'Others did more than I did...'
'If I wouldn't have done it, others would have...'
'It would have happened without me, anyway...'
'It would have been worse if I hadn't done it...'
'I had nothing to do with it...'
'I wash my hands off it, others are responsible...'
'I didn't know about it...'
'I just did what I was told...'
'I had no choice...'

Some of these evasions may remind you of your childhood, perhaps not the most ethical phase of a person's life. None of these pleas really absolves an adult from moral responsibility, of course. That is why in case of a moral lapse you always hear a few of these excuses used together. As if they would add up to exoneration.

The question is whether designers really have so much influence that it is fair to burden them with complete responsibility for any design. They are just one link in a whole chain of development activities within an organisation, which also bears responsibility. It could be argued that the role of designer is not a good basis for exercising this moral responsibility. It is much better to distance the argument from roles within organisations, and talk about this issue as a human being. Real moral responsibility is indeed personal, and it should be exercised on a personal basis. Informally objecting to a questionable development is anyone's responsibility. But this is just the first step. What if your opposition doesn't work? Do you then have the duty to undermine a morally objectionable development? Perhaps you do.

DESIGN IN
THE REAL WORLD

DESIGN AS A WAY
OF THINKING

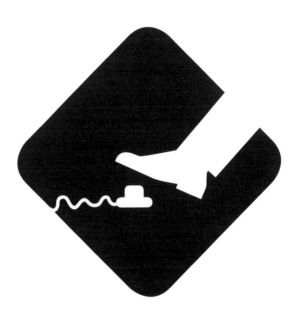

'EVERYTHING IS DESIGN'

There is a clear trend in many professions to see their work as 'designing'. For instance, managers now 'design' company policies, and in education, teachers design a curriculum. This always confuses me – I tend to take it as a compliment towards the design profession and feel appreciated. On the other hand, it makes me feel very uneasy.

As any reader of this book will have realised by now, designing is one of the vaguest and most complex ways of problem solving that a homo sapiens can experience. Just saying that a profession is 'like design' implies that its problems are about as unstructured and difficult as they can be. So, likening something to design is not a solution, it is just a way to rephrase the problem in even wider terms.

This is not to say that using design as a metaphor couldn't be useful in many fields. Designers' open, creative, solution-focussed way of working is very valuable in fields that have suffered from an overly rational approach. And some of the tricks and methods that designers use could surely benefit people in many professions. This is clearly illustrated by another way in which design spreads through society. These days, you encounter people with a design background in all kinds of jobs, who use their design thinking to solve the problems they face. And it works!
It is a pity that these people don't normally call themselves designers. That would really help put the design profession on the map.

APPLYING DESIGN THINKING

The application of 'design thinking' is not only limited to the synthesis of new ideas through techniques like brainstorming. The peculiar kind of creative analysis that is associated with design thinking can help us to comprehend the world in a fresh way.

The functional thinking of design has direct parallels in the natural world, where organisms are 'designed' to function optimally in their environment. Paul Colinvaux has demonstrated this in considering the 'design problem' of plant life in the middle of the ocean. The problem for life in the ocean is that the ocean is a kind of desert, with enormous amounts of nutrients that sink down deep because they are heavier than water. Sunlight that is needed to power life is only available in the top few meters of water. So the design problem becomes: how to bring these two elements, energy and nutrients, together? Colinvaux shows that this design problem has two solutions: enormous floating plants that have a large leaf area to support very long roots that hang down to reach the nutrients, or very small plants that circulate, bathing in light on the top layer of the sea, and then sinking down towards the nutrients. As it turns out, the giant plants with long roots actually exist in the Sargasso Sea, and the second design solution we know as the algae that form the basis of all life in the sea.

Design thinking helps to understand the man-made world in a similar fashion. By looking at things with a designers' eye, you get an idea of the reasoning and design process behind them. This reveals not only 'how things work', but also the 'why' behind them. Design is a way of looking, of being more actively involved in the world than most people. You are never content with how things appear. It is impossible to be bored when you are a designer.

SEEING AS...

Seeing other professions as design provides the practitioners within these professions with new tools for analysis and synthesis, and it shifts the focus away from thinking about the problem towards thinking about solutions.

This can be very helpful – but the 'old' and 'new' approaches easily clash. This can be illustrated by a study that was done into the development of prostheses, where doctors and designers work together in multidisciplinary development teams. The major cultural problem within these teams is that doctors are used to a position of absolute authority, and that they are used to make a quick, single diagnosis of a medical problem. Designers don't have this sort of mindset at all, they need to play around with several options before the problem is understood properly and the solutions that are generated start really 'fitting' the problem to their satisfaction. As a consequence, the meetings that were meant to be design sessions kept being interrupted because the doctors walked away, thinking they were finished after they had delivered their initial analysis. This to the amazement of the designers, who had not even begun...

To foster a more open way of problem solving, some design abilities should be spread more broadly throughout society. And this is beginning to happen. Design is now seen as one of the basic ways of thinking that a person needs to function in the modern world. As a consequence, design is now beginning to be taught in high schools throughout the world.

MEDIEVAL THINKING

The philosopher Michel Foucault describes how in the Middle Ages, the world was experienced in a completely different way. Things that we now view as being unrelated were, at that time, considered to be intimately connected.

For one thing, people believed that words and objects really corresponded to each other – that there was something inherently lionny about the word 'lion' and that a plant that looked like a brain (a cabbage, for instance) could be used as a medicine that was good for your brain. The object of medieval science was to identify all these connections, and incorporate them into a grand scheme of creation. God was considered to be the Great Thinker in the background who had conceived the world in this coherent way. It was only in the Renaissance that people began hesitantly, haltingly, to split things up. In the Age of Enlightenment reason and analysis reigned supreme. The world was cleanly laid out in different categories and subdivisions, clearly discernable from one another.

Designers tend to think in terms of finding or making connections. They are inclined to use associations and analogies to create new possibilities for solutions. Designers are basically medieval in the way they think.

DESIGN IN
THE REAL WORLD

DESIGN
AND SOCIETY

IDEOLOGY

What do designers believe in these days? The era of grand ideologies is now past. They have all collapsed over the same issue: the world is too complex to be captured in a single model. The ideologies which have survived the longest are those that used their dictatorial powers to organise their corner of the world to comply with the model. But even these 'paradises' unraveled after a while.

This 'end of utopia' also holds true in design. Would any designer today believe that their work has eternal value? That this new design is a breakthrough, that we finally know how to make things? Forever? If you read the ideological literature of design, like the manifesto of the De Stijl (The Style) movement in the 1920s, you find that this is what they claim. With enormous pathos and drama. Fanaticism. Their aim was a new abstract Art which would be universally understood. And they believed they had achieved this. That is why they called themselves The Style, not A Style. Absolute truth in art and design. We can't really imagine it now.

The last design style that possibly acted as a complete ideology was functionalism. This style is sober, unadorned, with attention to proportions, simplicity and clarity in construction and image. Order and harmony. There is an ideology behind this, a complete view of the world and people's needs. But functionalism has faded, and it was succeeded by a counter-movement that is much more ambiguous. The liberation from functionalism came in the guise of various styles that stressed ornamentation, historical metaphors and exuberant colours. In fact, this also liberated us from the whole idea of a single dominant style. We now live and work in an inspiring chaos of subcultures and diverse styles. This is a relief after the pressure of all those Ideologies that were much too grandiose and all-inclusive.

Something is gained – but something is also lost in the end of ideology. An ideology like functionalism helps a designer make consistent decisions, which are based upon a coherent set of arguments. Too extreme maybe, too one-sided. But as a designer you need *something* to go on.

AFTER IDEOLOGY

The end of ideology poses special problems for the training of designers. What can you teach students, except that anything is possible and everything probably has some value? How can you say something is bad, except on the level of craft or technical execution? How can you build a curriculum which compares with the sheer power of the Bauhaus? Or are we forever beyond that? Should design schools be institutes that only teach their students basic skills, because we aren't sure about anything else?

A lot of schools seem to be going in that direction: everything students produce is basically OK, as long as they can defend it. That is the politically correct way of dealing with this problem. Very humane, but quite fatal to design quality.

Students are, by definition, the absolute beginners in a field. We should not immediately burden them with the responsibility of developing their own set of fundamentals. Of course, students always have opinions about everything, but more often than not these are just a collection of things the students have heard and liked. As a tutor in a 'modern' design school, you are supposed to take these ideas seriously and try to discuss them. But if there is no firm ground underlying the students' opinions, those discussions go nowhere.

What you miss is the drive and energy of a real argument over solidly grounded fundamentals. This alone is reason enough to plead for renewed radicalism in design schools. If students cannot be expected to have a coherent set of interesting opinions, then the school and teachers should have them. If they, too, fail to take a position and defend it, relativism will rule. And relativists are always right, of course. Unfortunately, that doesn't lead to the interesting designs we are all looking for.

ROLES FOR DESIGN

Design can play a role in shaping the future of our society. The larger processes of societal change are often seen as inevitable, almost as natural processes that beset humanity. And it is true that these processes are difficult to start, stop or steer. They are also much too complicated to design directly: they involve complex technical, social and cultural issues over long periods of time. It is hard to imagine what a country will look like in twenty years.

Yet, these large scale processes can be moulded. In Holland right now there is an issue of agriculture disappearing from some parts of the countryside, to be replaced by 'nature'. There are pilot projects underway to see how this transition will work, what the change will mean to the community and how the more intensively concentrated forms of agriculture can be redesigned (as industries, not as farms) to avoid a negative impact on the environment. Our influence on the landscape is total. Therefore, we need to start thinking about it as a design problem. This does not mean that we can design the future completely, but it means that we have to use design thinking to avoid the unwanted consequences of our decisions.

The solution-focussed strategies of designers are incredibly valuable for raising the right issues and making scenarios of things to come. Design is not just about the creation of things, it is a way of thinking that can help to shape the future.

DESIGN VERSUS THE REAL WORLD

While design is related to our hopes for the future, it must also combat defeatism about where we are heading. Humanity is realising the global scale of its impact. We have reached the limits of our planet.

Visionary designer and design educator Victor Papanek published 'Design for the Real World', back in 1971. In this book he criticised much of the consumerism he saw around him, and in projects demonstrated how one can design things that are better for the world: improved quality, longer lasting, and addressing the real needs of people. As an example he pointed to a whole array of low budget products that were especially designed for the developing world. Not naive, well intended designs for 'those people down there' but clever products that are better suited to the local circumstances.

He also recognised that as a single designer you are powerless against major developments like the depletion of fossil fuels. But the fact that such problems are so overpoweringly huge doesn't mean that the solution may not lie in many small design improvements. Papanek passionately urges his readers to make their profession part of the answer to these problems. This brings a whole new set of criteria to any design project. Of course it is easier to ignore this appeal, and to remain part of the problem.

BEING LOW IN THE PECKING ORDER

Design is still not regarded as a substantive profession. People find what you do very interesting, but taking it seriously is quite another matter. So you keep defending the importance of design, and struggle for recognition. Why is it that design is invariably placed so low on people's hierarchy of professions?

In Western society, there is a kind of pecking order of professions that is based upon an ancient view of how humanity develops knowledge. The view is that Knowledge (with a capital K) is generated by fundamental sciences, and then applied by technologists. The technology must then be translated into usable objects, by people called designers. The ranking is clear: the more applied, the less 'pure' the knowledge, and so a lower status is conveyed to the people using that knowledge.
This odd hierarchical thinking is not limited to the technical side of design either: graphic design and formgiving are often described as 'applied arts'. Clearly, these are lowly occupations when compared to 'real art'.

This absurd hierarchy is based upon a mistaken view of the design professions. It is not true that designers only translate 'technology' or 'art' into usable goods. Design is a separate profession, and not a derivative of anything else. You don't have to be a failed artist or scientist to become a designer.

The only way to combat these unfortunate, deep-rooted misconceptions is to develop our own heritage of Design, to compete with Art and Science. We should clarify what design is and explain its role in society. Perhaps we need a Nobel Prize for design.

DESIGN IN
THE REAL WORLD

PAST

CULTURE AND DESIGN

In the wonderfully poetic 1933 essay 'In Praise of Shadows', the Japanese writer Jun'ichirō Tanizaki describes the culture and aesthetics of traditional Japan. He describes how the traditional Japanese house is constructed with layers of paper screens, making the outside rooms very light, while the inside rooms become darker and darker. In this shadowy world lived the women, with their traditional makeup of whitened faces and green lips. The inner rooms also held the folding screens, opulently decorated with gold so that they would sparkle in the darkness by the flame of a candle.

Tanizaki's sensitive description evokes a complete world of austere but subtle aesthetics, that has long since disappeared (the essay was written as a protest against the introduction of electric lights).

Design is an integral part of the culture of a country or region. What is 'typically Scandinavian' about Swedish and Danish furniture? Can the aesthetics and value systems that define this kind of furniture design be transposed to other products like cars, machines or software? Do we even want that?

Many of the decisions you make in design are rather implicit, and partially determined by the culture in which you are working. Even if you work methodically and use 'objective' evaluation techniques to explicitly choose between design concepts, you have already made many implicit decisions in the creation of those concepts.

WHAT'S NEW?

Every designer should browse through the Sears, Roebuck & Company mail order catalogues of a century ago. Take the 1908 catalogue. What do you find in there? Everything. Really everything a person needed for a comfortable life. Complete houses, built ready for occupancy ($ 725 for a nice two-storey wooden house, with a choice of doorknobs and hearth decoration), completely modern looking bathrooms, eyeglasses (with an eye chart in the catalogue), fashion, Bibles, carriages and carts, pianos (with the patented mouse-proof pedal), underwear, toys, cans of food, medicine – absolutely everything. The catalogue was the only outlet for Sears, Roebuck & Company. It contained 1100 pages, and was distributed for free in an edition of 600,000 copies (!). It was a huge success. Everybody knew Sears – The Cheapest Supply House on Earth.

A century later, this catalogue gives a designer the humbling impression that everything has already been done. Human needs do not change that much, and the products which fulfil those needs don't really change either, despite all our efforts to the contrary. What are the differences between then and now? Electricity was not widely available, and there were no electric motors – so all tools were hand tools. The fridge had no cooling pump, but a block of ice. But these are just minor differences in operating principles, providing essentially the same functionality.

The only product categories we have now that really provide us with a different functionality than there was around a hundred years ago, are the computers and mobile phones of the recent information revolution. They are still new to us, and they are set to change our lives dramatically. More so than all the design work in the past century.

CYCLES AND PROGRESS

The past centuries have seen a linear view of history, at least in the Western world. In this view, humanity is developing in a positive direction, improving in every way, presumably advancing towards some state of ultimate happiness, 'the end of history'.

That vision was rocked by World Wars, and has faded in the last half of the 20th century. Utopia is forever beyond reach. But still, we keep developing. The things we make are getting better and better, but never seem to reach an end state, if only because our own inventiveness also opens up new needs and possibilities. And the advancements tend to get out of balance in all sorts of new and interesting ways. This gives the never-ending story of progress something of a cyclical feeling. Problems we haven't seen for ages tend to reappear in a different setting.

It looks like the advances in technology easily outrun our capacity to integrate them in our lives. Faster computers will lead to new communication possibilities for which there is no cultural framework (What is the etiquette for mobile phone use?), and society will have to develop standards for the safe and acceptable use of these new technologies. An additional problem is that the changes we are experiencing move at widely different speeds. Office buildings can last for 50 years, but our way of working in an office is transforming quite dramatically, on a timescale of every few years. So flexibility must become paramount in architecture. If not, offices and houses will be out of date by the time they are finished. Buildings will have to 'learn' and adapt as society changes at a furious pace.

THE EVOLUTION OF THINGS

Designers are much too busy to think beyond the design projects they are working on. But it does pay to delve into the history of the things we are developing, to know the history we are a part of.

The trouble is that much of the historical record is concerned with creating a story of progress, but that reality was always more complicated and interesting. If we take the simple example of the evolution of the bicycle, then it seems inevitable that the current model, the Rover Safety Bike of 1884, would overcome its onetime competitors, the 'penny-farthing' bike (huge front wheel, small one at the back) and the tricycle. But history shows that these three different bike concepts co-existed, side by side, for many years, with each one of them neatly capturing about one third of the market. The penny-farthing satisfied the speeding daredevils, the tricycle suited the ladies, and the Safety Bike was for everyone else. Many people were convinced that it would just be a matter of time before the tricycle was the only commercially available cycle. Even knowing this, it is hard to ignore our knowledge of the outcome and not be convinced that the Safety Bike would win. It is always easy to see which features and criteria were the most important in this selection processes, because other aspects seem insignificant now.

Although the past may seem predestined with the benefit of hindsight, there is nothing very logical to us about the 'now' we are living in. Design is permeated by this uncertainty about the future. There are three disastrous reactions to this uncertain future: procrastination, non-committal design and throw-away design. The sentiment behind procrastination is that the future will be much clearer if we just wait a little. Of course, the moment for action will never come. In non-committal design you stay as neutral as possible, making something bland and grey that won't please nor offend anyone. This must be the most popular strategy since we are surrounded by such objects. The third approach is the most wasteful: to design for the present only, and to expect that the object will be quickly replaced.

THE CURRENT REVOLUTION

We live on top of the past, in a fleeting moment we call 'now'. We are mostly occupied with the future, but we do not know which of the objects we see around us really points towards the future. The past and the future are both present in the now.

We do not only try to build a picture of the future, we also reinterpret what has gone before. We selectively reinvent the past and rewrite history to construct a coherent story. This even happens to something as future-oriented and visionary as the development of company mission statements. Many of them are more about changing the past than creating a new plan for the future. We have a deeply felt need to fashion a consistent story of our lives, and preferably one that develops positively, onward and upward. We also tend to experience the time we live in as a revolutionary one. The current situation always seems to be a radical break with the past. This cannot be true, but we like to think so anyway.

Still, today we are witnessing very big changes in our lives, because of the information revolution. Completely new technologies, services and classes of products are being developed. They concentrate on communication, information, entertainment, culture and services. To complicate life further, we are also experiencing the chaotic growing pains of globalisation that results from these technologies.

The extent of these changes makes it very hard to predict what the future will look like. These are interesting times for the companies we work in: there are great opportunities for success as well as failure. Prophets of all sorts spring up, and we do not know which of them will be right.

DESIGN IN THE REAL WORLD

DESIGN DEBATES

THE NEED FOR DEBATE

Until now, this book has discussed design as an activity, a way of think-ing, a social phenomenon, a managerial problem, or as something to be learned. All these subjects dealt with the shape of the design activity, but not with the content of what we design. But we cannot ignore the object of design forever, because designing is all about the creation of quality in a design.

The debate how quality should be defined takes place among design-ers within all design fields. It is a debate in words, fought out in books, exhibitions and design magazines. It is also argued with designs, since many designs provoke other designers to react with a design of their own. This is a huge area of contradictory philosophies, arguments and opinions. The next pages of this book will look into some aspects of these debates, such as the form and level of discussions, some classic themes that represent fundamental divisions, and the way design controversies get resolved.

But the only way to really understand the issues, and to profit from the discussions in your area of design, is to participate. So, jump right in.

Still, why do we need debate about design? Why can't we just do design, and avoid all the endless pseudo-theoretical discussions about what a 'good' design is, if we are never going to come to any conclusions? Is it necessary, or even useful, to discuss design at all? There is a case to be made for design debate. In theorizing and discussing design, we try to make sense of an immensely chaotic and dynamic field. We build up a collective account of design, which can help make our design knowledge understandable to ourselves and transferable to the next generation of designers. But we should realise that we build these edifices of design knowledge on very subjective foundations, and that all these histories and theories only have temporary value. Eternal truths are not to be found. We have to allow that others, who also care about design, can see things in a radically different way. They may be right, from a completely different perspective, and there may be inspiration in that.

THE SUCCESSION OF STYLES

Many design discussions center around the notion of Style. A style is simply a kind of coherent approach to problems and a preference for a certain type of solutions, that serves as a basis while designing. As a designer you have a style, whether you want it or not. This style is always personal, but the personal styles of designers tend to be aligned in a period, and take part in a general Style in the culture of the day.

These styles change over time, with new styles emerging to react against the existing ones. One can see this as a debate about style, where the new tries to prove the old wrong. In this game of action, reaction and counter-reaction, some design aspects and priorities come to the fore while others decline. There is something of a cyclical nature about this, with styles returning after a number of years. If the succession of styles proves anything, it is that in design there is seldom one ultimate answer that will stand the test of time. There are just so many possibilities to solve a functional problem, and there is so much freedom in interpretation and form that we should be able to go on designing forever.

But there are some designs that do not seem to participate in this Ferris wheel. They stand the test of time because they have a certain special quality. Is this quality of being 'a classic' a historical and social phenomenon, or is it inherent in any particularly good design? I want to believe that for a real 'classic' the originality and some indefinable quality of the design itself are the most important factors.

But every brand today wants to become a 'classic', and takes the social route to this status by calling itself 'classic' in its advertising campaign (and inventing some bogus history). They keep shouting desperately that they are a classic, lest they be forgotten. Real Classics speak for themselves.

OBSOLESCENCE

The succession of styles has been condemned as an unnecessary and wasteful phenomenon. And it has definitely been a terrible waste of resources. In the boom-years of the fifties and sixties, US carmakers tried to entice the public to buy a new car every year ('the '61 Mercury is the Best Car Ever Built'). This incredible era of affluence and throwaway goods has long since passed. We are not so naive anymore about the effect we have on this planet.

Still, we need to find ways to make better use of our resources. The 'Eternally Yours' movement of recent years has moved beyond the physical durability of products (don't make throwaway goods) into what they call the psychological durability of a design. This simply means that we hold on to the things we like, the things we can relate to. We use and enjoy them a lot longer, and inadvertently save the environment. To increase psychological durability, we need more appealing and less superficial designs with a certain inbuilt flexibility.

Yet, we will never stop designing new things for people. Some level of change seems to be natural, inspiring and have an innate value. There is something in human nature that makes us crave stimulation in our environment. But new things quickly loose their stimulating ability. It is amazing how quickly we get used to a new shape in cars, for instance. Today's spectacular 'concept cars' will be the boring standard saloon five years from now. What is slightly worrying is that in this MTV age of sensory overload we get so used to rapid development, that we might need these thrills quicker and quicker.

DOES FORM FOLLOW FUNCTION?

Functionalism (or Modernism) is the dominant style of the last century. This style is still very much with us today, the old adage Form Follows Function, coined by the architect Louis Sullivan in 1896 (!), still looms in the background of many discussions about design, in various design fields.

The functionalist drive for 'pure', functional design is very much alive. The determination to do away with 'unnecessary' ornament gave rise to a refreshing rethinking of the world around us in the Bauhaus era and the creation of a 'machine aesthetics'. But functionalists and modernists have interpreted Form Follows Function very strictly, and accompanied it with a very limited view of what the function of a design is. Le Corbusier, in defining a house as 'a machine for living in', limited himself to what he saw as the pure functions, the physical aspects of 'living'. Which makes his houses singularly cold and uninhabitable. It is the concept of meditative purity that is found in monasteries, but not in normal life.

The real problem with functionalism doesn't lie in these harmless, extreme, more or less theoretical examples of great designers and architects who are exploring a style. The real problem lies in the real world, where it turned out that modernism was cheap to build. The modernist ideas were taken up enthusiastically by developers, and they have given us complete cities built in this style. Cold cityscapes full of austere 'functionality'. This degenerated brand of functionalism has become so common that it is almost the default style. It is always the cheapest, and you need many good arguments to convince a client to move beyond the bare necessities.

As the great functionalists say: 'Less is more' (Mies von der Rohe). But does less make us happier?

HONESTY AND INTEGRITY IN DESIGN

Design debates are all about defining what quality is. These discussions are often quite metaphorical, because apparently we lack the vocabulary to talk about design quality directly. In these debates, the objects of design are often given human attributes, introducing both a handy metaphor and some confusion about whether the discussion about human qualities and about things can be treated as being equal.

For instance, designers talk about the 'honest use of materials' as a value in itself, which means that a design should show the way it was made. This 'honesty' also extends to an absolute ban on ornament, dating back to the machine aesthetics of the Bauhaus.
 The honesty metaphor allows this style to masquerade as a fundamental moral standpoint, and its followers no doubt saw it this way. In terms of humanity, honesty is one of our basic positive values. You should be honest. But, as my design professor once said when I tried to bring this point up as an argument in a discussion, defending a mechanism that was not protected from interfering fingers: 'You can also be too honest...'. And there we were, dropping out of the safe realm of abstract discourse back onto the slippery slope of reality.

Likewise, terms like 'integrity' are used to represent the 'wholeness' or 'rightness' in a design. We cannot be too careful with these metaphors, because introducing loaded terms like these can cloud a discussion enormously.

GOOD TASTE

In areas of especially personal and subjective knowledge, like formgiving and aesthetics, there is a small group of opinion leaders who define good taste. This shadowy circle wields enormous influence over the design community. This group used to be made up of people with a high social status, the 'high society'. But nowadays the social status of designers has increased to the extent that a star designer can be his own opinion leader. The things he makes are good and interesting, because *he* says so... Which is, of course, a wonderful racket, and many students aspire to this comfortable status. This is real 'success' in a social sense.

This elite frowns upon most of the designs that are made for 'normal' people, and dismiss them as commonplace, cheap and conservative. And of course they are often all of these things. The preferred qualities of 'normal' objects lie in unspectacularly fulfilling their function with a reasonable price. These unheroic designs make up 99% of the economy, and are the silent helpers of mankind. One could argue that the real value of elite design lies in the extent to which it can inspire this great mass of design. Not in its own overblown existence in design shops. If Haute Couture has a reason to exist at all, it should be because of the way it inspires Prêt-à-Porter and the broader confection industry.

THE THREE QUALITIES

The design discipline implicitly contains three incommensurable view-points about what is 'good' and 'bad', three fundamentally different ways of defining Quality.
- Some designers and design critics tend to be utilitarian – they would say that a design that people want and buy is, by definition, a good design. For them, success is King.
- Others would argue that a design can be intrinsically good, regardless of the reaction of the public. They say that Quality is deeply engrained in the things we make, and not dependent on the whims of public opinion. They cherish the notion of 'design classics' for this reason.
- Still others argue that designs that are made in correspondence with certain virtues (like simplicity, honesty, care, 'showing the hand of the maker'), and that designs derive their real Quality from this.

Which of these do you subscribe to?

In all situations where a design is judged, these considerations potentially come into play, but they are seldom expressed at this fundamental level. Too often the decisions we make in design are cast as a matter of pragmatic choice between alternatives. But this is not true: the three kinds of Quality outlined above are silently lurking behind every design decision! The three Qualities each not only lead to fundamentally different ways of defining what is 'a good design', but also to different views on the approach a designer should take, and on the motivation that a designer might have for producing a particular design outcome.

The realisation that our designs have three different kinds of Quality can lead to much deeper and more interesting debates in the design arena.

EVERLASTING DEBATES AND THEIR RESOLUTION

Because of the way most design debates originate and perpetuate, you can be sure that people are never going to agree. Their fate can be summed up by Andy Warhol's black remark that *'you can never tell anybody anything anyway...'*

The reason design disputes are so tough is that, with design being such an open and underdetermined profession, there are many approaches one can take to understanding design, and many ways to describe what good design is. These differing viewpoints are rooted in the fundamentally different ways people look at the world. Rationalists against Intuition, Problem Solvers against Learners, Idealists against Pragmatists... But design is seldom discussed at that level, the debate usually centers on the application of these fundamental differences in design practice. Because they do not go back to the point where their differences originate, such arguments can never be resolved.

Maybe that should not even be the main goal of the debate, since it is a good way to concentrate thoughts and to clarify a subject. The philosopher Emmanuel Levinas has turned the whole debate within philosophy on its head by observing that all of philosophy is about being right, and convincing others that you are right. He claims that this is not always the most interesting thing to do. He proposes a 'philosophy of the other', which focuses on finding ways to understand the other, instead of trying to overpower him with arguments. This could be an interesting approach for a new, more productive type of design discussion.

As it is, the fundamental differences at the root of design debates mean that they have no resolution. Old debates never really die, they just fade away into irrelevance.

DESIGN IN
THE REAL WORLD

FUTURE

SCIENCE WILL FIX IT

The height of popular belief in the unlimited powers of science and technology lies behind us, in the middle of the twentieth century.

Projects that were seen as positive visions of the future included good ideas like improving the delivery time of mail by using intercontinental missiles, and closing off the Mediterranean Sea at Gibraltar, so that it would evaporate to provide valuable new land for agriculture. The famines of sub-Saharan Africa were also seen as a technical problem. The water that is so badly needed for irrigation is present, but is hidden deep below the sand. The easiest way to get it is to drop a nuclear bomb, somewhere in southern Libya, which would provide a wonderful round lake (at the time, nuclear fallout was seen as a slightly more bothersome variety of the common cold). These were heroic times for engineering. Huge construction projects were dreamt up by engineers, and some of them, like the Aswan Dam in Egypt, were really built. And we would never have walked on the moon if it weren't for this enormous confidence in science and technology.

These excitingly optimistic times, where technical fixes were going to be found for everything, are long gone. What happened? The consequences have caught up with us. Nowadays we are quite busy trying to fix them instead of reaching for the stars. And rightly so.

TECHNOPHILIA AND TECHNOPHOBIA

Too much uncertainty in how we should deal with the future is fatal. People teeter between a dangerous confidence that Science Will Fix It (Technophilia) and a paralysing fear that they will be the victims of developments that science and technology have brought down upon them (Technophobia).

The truth is that, until recently, science has more or less solved our problems. But that was in a fairly stable world that had not yet been confronted with challenges on the global scale of today. The basic issue now is how you can approach such huge crises at all, except by saying that we are unfortunately running out of planet.

The problem is that these crises are defined and analysed as global concerns, but that the answers will have to come from many small local developments, the benefits of which then hopefully add up to a complete solution. The ball is firmly in our court, as individual designers, entrepreneurs and consumers.

TRENDS AND PLANS

Predictions are hard to make. Companies therefore prefer not to depend upon a single statement of 'the future will be like this', but on a range of scenarios.

These scenarios are made in such a way that the main controlling variables can be modified to see how the general picture changes. They take the form of 'if the population keeps growing at this rate, then... if the oil price triples, then...'. In this way a whole network of interconnected forecasts are built up. It is also possible to enter the newest trends to see whether they will indeed lead to the different image of the future. You can discover what the chances are of a certain event becoming reality, depending on the many variables. You model the world and try to understand the dynamics of future development so you can anticipate it. We must keep planning, at all costs. We are lost and powerless if we stop investigating the future.

Trendwatchers make good money out of this uncertainty and fear of the future. They specialise in self-fulfilling prophecies: what they claim will be the new fashion, will probably become the fashion because they say so, since companies listen to them. Trendwatchers can become trendsetters. As a designer, you ignore them at your peril.

DESIGN FOR DEBATE

The UK designers Anthony Dunne and Fiona Raby are convinced that design has a great and seldom used potential to appeal to people's imagination and to spark thoughtful discussion. They dislike the fact that most design is completely driven by commerce. They see a much deeper intellectual value in design's ability to trigger debate, discussion and arguments about our possible futures.

Traditionally the role of initiating debates that reflect on the human condition, our values and the meaning of life, has been assigned to the fine arts or other art forms like film. But Dunne and Raby argue that this doesn't work anymore – when you walk into a modern art museum or go to a movie, you enter with the anticipation of having an experience, maybe even being shocked. This makes you virtually impervious to that experience. You step into a world where your everyday life is put on hold and your sensitivity is blunted. You are not yourself anymore, you have become an observer.

But a design can catch you off guard: it is out there in the real world, and your initial reaction will come from your real self. So when you encounter a design that contains an unexpected layer of meaning, you are compelled to stop and think about this design's message to the world. Anthony Dunne and Fiona Raby have built an extensive oeuvre by designing in this way: they call it 'design for debate'. For instance, they created a beautiful stuffed plaything for children in the shape of a mushroom cloud, so kids can get used to the reality of a nuclear explosion at a tender age... That HURTS!

To design for debate is an extremely subtle art: it is comparatively easy to make designs that shock, but this will only result in people rejecting your design outright without thinking about it. It is really hard to create a design that is intuitively attractive to people but that, on reflection, reveals hidden messages that will make people feel uneasy and cause them to think again. So the stuffed mushroom cloud is a well made toy, a very attractive object, really – when you look at it without thinking.

DESIGN AND ACADEMIA

All around the world, design schools are moving into academia. In my opinion this development is long overdue: the questions that designers are dealing with have for years already been of a complexity, depth and intellectual interest that an academic training has become a necessity. The development of an 'academic' side to the design profession is the logical next step in the evolution of the field. But we need to be careful: you cannot simply transpose a professional field which aims at the creation of value in designs into an academic environment where the accumulation of objective knowledge is the leading value.

Some design schools are so eager to establish themselves in the academic community that they have fallen into the trap of trying to adhere to the criteria of a 'classic' academic discipline. In their desperation to blend in, they have attached all kinds of 'scientific research' to their design projects. This 'scientific research' seldom results in an improvement of the quality of the design outcome – it actually detracts from it, because the energy of the student is drawn away from the design work towards a strange obsession with trying to 'prove' decisions at every step of the design project. This pressure to provide evidence for everything they do is absurd – design is a creative discipline in which a designer proposes and experiments, and in which there is very little that can be justified before you actually make an experimental design and reflect upon it. This stress on *a priori* analytical thinking and up-front proof diminishes the openness and playfulness that is needed to arrive at a great design. This 'scientification' of design easily leads to a kind of halfway house: mediocre design results, propped up by a report with painfully unconvincing 'scientific' evidence that pathetically tries to explain how good the solution is.

Don't get me wrong: the complexities of design in this day and age mean that there is a great need for academic designers that are able to carry out research, and to integrate scientific knowledge into their design practice. But we need to develop a new mode of 'design research' that is more suited to fruitfully feed into the design project than traditional 'scientific research'. We also have to explain that design is fundamentally different from 'classic' academic disciplines, and to demonstrate that design is an activity that in itself can be performed at an academic level.

GLOBALISATION

Design, the creation of the new, is a good barometer of society. In its search for innovation Design responds acutely and hungrily to the forces of new technological developments and socio-cultural change. In doing so, it has become a force in itself, articulating, shaping and expressing fundamental shifts in our ideas and values.

The exciting new possibilities in communication and information technology have changed our lives forever, in many different ways. Designers have almost been taken aback by the speed and impact of this revolution, and some repercussions of the Brave New World have not completely sunk in yet. The sheer idea of globalisation is mind-boggling. When I was educated as a product designer in Holland, that training was implicitly geared towards the development of products to meet the needs of Dutch industry at the time – mostly small and medium sized manufacturing companies that produced for a local market. Having a broad view of all aspects of a product was deemed important, and the ability to single-handedly integrate all of these aspects into the final design was the main aim of our training.

Since then the work of the designer has shifted from being this lone creator and integrator towards becoming a contributor in a team design effort, and the whole world has become a potential partner in producing, marketing and using the designs we make. Thus it has become much more important for a designer to realise where his strength lies – as a specialist in a single aspect of the design field, or in integrating specific aspects – and to position himself on a very big international stage. The ability to create and function in networks of like-minded people (aka 'communities of practice') has become a new key skill in functioning as a designer. Globalisation has impressed upon us the new challenge of having to explicitly develop our own network of contacts, an inner-net that interacts with many others.

COPYCAT

The unfolding of the world into a global market has provoked a new interest in the development of a strong and unique local identity. Designers and design agencies alike are having to think long and hard about what their strengths are, and how they are going to display these strengths on an ever expanding stage.

Design being the complicated and broad profession that it is, these strengths can range from being knowledgeable about a certain kind of design content, to design methods or the ability to work with a certain advanced technology. But we must be wary: most advantages are very short-lived, and any success is hard to maintain in a world that is overrun with opportunists. Intellectual property is becoming harder and harder to defend (in the end, the only real defence against the theft of your ideas is to have lots of them).

Within this global cat-and-mouse game, knowledge can be transferred with lightning speed and special skills are very hard to hold on to. But cultural factors are becoming more important than ever. The complex mix of values and meanings that we have developed over the years in a society, have proven to be invaluable – and hard to copy. Thus we see that, paradoxically, globalisation has led designers and towards introspection and soul-searching to define the core cultural value of their design identity.

Knowing this identity is, of course, only the beginning – how do you express something as complex as a cultural identity in an age where attention spans are short and the Image is everything? The Dutch designer Marcel Wanders may be an interesting case in point. In 1996, he created the 'Knotted Chair' (see page 187). A bold design statement, which has been adopted as an icon of its age. The chair has been included in many books about design, and has been incorporated into museum collections the world over. As a piece of furniture design, we cannot call it a commercial success – very few were made (and it is still being produced in small numbers). But the image of the Knotted Chair has been copied millions of times, and Marcel Wanders has been able to develop commercially successful products that capture some of the conceptual magic of his visionary design. He has established an inimitable identity.

THE DESIGNER AND THE PYRAMID

The wealth in the world is increasing. We have never had it so good. This means that the design sector will have to adapt, and grow towards catering for a radically different set of values. The Maslov pyramid could be helpful as a framework for explaining what I mean by this. The Maslov pyramid is a simple ranking of human needs and values. At the bottom are the basic necessities of life like food and water. One layer up we find more complex needs that are still related to our physical existence like safety and sex. Above that, social and cultural needs begin to play a part: we need friendship, we need to feel loved, to belong to a community, and we need to have the freedom to develop our own identity. At the top of the original pyramid Maslov put 'self realisation' – which has always been a much-contested statement.

This simple hierarchy of needs can help us designers appreciate what values we are implicitly aiming for. With more and more people becoming quite secure about the fulfilment of their basic needs, society is slowly moving up the Maslov pyramid. You can see this quite clearly when you realise what people in the richer parts of the world tend to spend their money on: expensive cars (identity), holidays (friendship, inspiration, relaxation), and communication tools like computers and mobile phones (again, friendship, community, etc). And there is an absolute boom in courses that help people find themselves, their innermost being – so self-realisation is surely up at the top somewhere.

One would expect designers to be very cognizant of these developments, and to search for ways to ride the wave of the Maslov pyramid. For many, this would mean leaving the old basis of their profession, which was serving the needs of the lower levels of the pyramid by largely functional designs, moving up towards designing for needs like friendship and inspiration. And because most of the higher level values and needs are about how we connect and live with each other, designers should perhaps leave the physical realm and become service designers. The future for design lies where society feels the greatest need.

DESIGN CONNECTS

Designers now often get involved in projects that deal with the socio-cultural values in the very highest reaches of the Maslov pyramid. These projects tend to be of such a complex nature that design work can no longer just be based on a naive personal understanding of the issues at hand.

The designer's traditional intuitive approach has to be augmented by a considerable amount of research in order to arrive at a deeper understanding of the social and cultural lives of the people they are designing for. Designers have to get beyond the easy assumptions about 'what people want', and really strive to understand what the culture of their users is: what do people value in their life, and how do they assign meaning to the world around them? And they have to get to grips with issues like social cohesion, inequality, rationality, (group)decision making and identity that influence the life of their users.

This kind of knowledge could be gained by designers studying scientific research that has been done on complex socio-cultural problem areas, or by reading novels that deal with these issues on a very concrete and human level. But that is not enough. All of this second-hand knowledge should be augmented by designers doing socio-cultural research themselves. The aim of such 'practice-led research' is not just to generate knowledge, but also to give designers they first-hand experience they need to feed their intuition. The detail and animation of a real-world experience will set the creative wheels spinning. We have to get out there.

THE CASE OF THE DISAPPEARING DESIGNER

Design as a clearly definable profession could be on the verge of disappearing.

This could just be the next step in the evolution of the design profession. If we take product design as an example, we can see that this design discipline came to the fore in the late 1800s as a separate profession because the industrial revolution made this specialisation necessary. The natural link between design and production that existed in the craft tradition was broken. Simultaneously, the need to civilise the otherwise crude objects of mass production led to the creation of the artist-designer, who applied their 'art' to the machine-made products of industrial scale manufacturing. After WWII, the continuing growth in complexity of the design field led to the creation of the 'integrated product designer'. This was a single designer whose expertise spanned the areas of form giving, ergonomics, technology, business and marketing, and whose role was to integrate these aspects into a product. Since then, the intricacies of the product design field proved too great for a single designer, leading to the rise of 'design teams' comprising individuals with different skills. In response to a further growth in complexity of the field, we have moved on to 'participatory design' (where users and stakeholders are consulted throughout the design project) and to 'collaborative design' (where users and stakeholders are actively involved in the creation of the design).

In collaborative design, the traditional position of 'the designer' as the great integrator and sole plan maker disappears, and design becomes a team effort which includes many different parties. Thus design is redefining itself again, and the borders of the profession are getting fuzzier all the time... Yet the core way designers think has withstood the tests of time, and is actually beginning to spread throughout society.

SOLVING THE UNSOLVABLE PROBLEM

We are living through a communication revolution (mobile phones, the internet) and find ourselves newly connected to innumerable people. This can enrich our lives enormously. But by networking our society we have inadvertently networked our problems as well. Thus the blessed state of hyper-connectedness is also the source of a fundamentally new kind of complex problem. Many important issues we face in today's society have become so complicated that they seem impervious to solution.

This forces us to reconsider the old ways of problem solving. Most of our 'traditional' problem solving strategies work reasonably well in an orderly universe: when problems appear we could isolate them in a relatively separate problem arena, abstract from the details of the concrete problem situation, decompose and analyse the sub-problems, and reach a conclusion in due course. If all else fails, we could use authority or power to 'simplify' the problem area by overruling some parties, and force a solution.

But this strategy does not work for today's problems: the enclosed 'mini-worlds' of our societies, economies and cultures have been replaced by a tangle of relationships within complex and overlapping networks, where power doesn't rest in one place, and truth there seems to have become a matter of perspective. Problems are so intimately related to each other (and there are so many dependencies between these interrelationships) that it is impossible to isolate one, no matter how hard you try. You see this happen all the time: governments, in particular, are very accustomed to a hierarchical and purely analysis-based way of problem solving (which they have organised in well-defined and reasonable government institutions). But they seem powerless to deal with the complex issues we face today, resulting in an endless parade of news items about botched decision making. And not only governments: companies and institutions all around the world have trouble dealing with the complexity of their problems. We desperately need to find a new way of tackling these complex, networked problems.

Design thinking could be part of the answer.

DESIGNING OUR WAY TO THE FUTURE

We know that we need to live more lightly on the earth. We urgently need to find a way to successfully manage our natural resources, and to meet the threat of global warming and pollution in the decades to come. Unfortunately, these 'physical' problems are exacerbated by the 'human' problems of our persistently unstable political landscape, widening cultural divides and the seemingly intractable problems of social inequality.

The evolutionary patterns of development which have brought us to this point may not be adequate for solving the problems we are facing today. People are beginning to realise that something has to change in the very way we deal with problems. More and more companies, governments and institutions are turning towards the field of design for help. Designers have naturally been dealing with complex, networked problems that involve multiple stakeholders for many years. Their 'design thinking' involves the creative exploration of problems and the creation of solutions that somehow overcome the paradoxes in the problem area that would be insurmountable using traditional problem solving. This is just what we need.

Thus the knowledge, skills and ways of thinking of designers could become increasingly important in the future. Designers themselves need to realise that they can use their design thinking in novel ways, moving far beyond the traditional design domains. We live in an interesting age.

A METAPHOR FOR DESIGN

METAPHORS WE LIVE BY

We always use metaphors to help us understand the world, because they are convenient simplifications that capture complex situations by likening them to more familiar ones. In this book I have used many metaphors to describe design: design as a balancing act, design as a conflict, design as a game, design as a puzzle, design as a conversation, design as a learning process... Each metaphor highlights different aspects of design and helps us to reflect on the subject as a whole.

But as designers, we also actively use metaphors in our work. If you embrace a metaphor, it heavily influences your response to a design situation. You 'live' a metaphor, in the sense that it shapes the way you work and how you deal with others. If we see design as a conflict, we could see the client as the enemy and our ideas and concepts as weapons to overcome resistance. Presentations and meetings become the battlegrounds. This metaphor can be useful in itself – design can be understood very much like an argument in some circumstances. But it can also be a self-fulfilling prophecy: the metaphors we live by influence our interaction with the outside world. If we adopt this metaphor of design-is-war, we are going to behave in a way that breeds resistance. We then create our own enemies. This may be completely unnecessary.

It is a good idea to observe other designers and try to imagine which metaphors they use to guide their behaviour. Fun, and extremely illuminating. For example, I know a young designer who looks at his design projects as friendly cooperations. When a project runs into trouble, and the client starts being difficult, he is genuinely surprised and upset. Big blue innocent eyes. In the face of that, it is hard for any client to stay angry.

DESIGN AS EXPLORATION

What would be a fruitful metaphor for looking at design? There are many possibilities, of course, some of which have been used in this book. But I particularly like to view design as an exploration.

Let's take this metaphor and describe it in detail to see what the statement 'design is exploration' leads to in terms of design knowledge, design strategies, design frames and in terms of the value judgements that designers make. All other metaphors can be analysed in a similar fashion, and it is useful to do this because it helps you to understand the metaphor you are currently living, and to explicitly choose the metaphor that is the most productive in a concrete situation.

What are the possibilities and limitations of seeing design as an exploration?

Picture yourself as a 19th Century explorer, setting out to find something of value (the source of the Nile?) in a cluttered landscape, say a jungle mountain range. So the first elements of the metaphor are an unknown territory, and wanting to go somewhere, but not being sure where. You can expect difficulties ahead, maybe even danger, but what will they be? There is a general direction you want to go in, but no trails. To find the easiest route, the landscape should be followed, and it may even have to be conquered. Deciding whether to climb a mountain, or go around it, are difficult choices to be made if you don't know their consequences. You basically have to forge ahead, but be ready to backtrack if your route becomes too difficult. You must also keep an eye on your limited resources and change your approach if they get irresponsibly low. Finally, any allies you might meet along the way could be very important.

This doesn't sound unlike design, does it? It is not a complete description of designing (for instance, design is much more complicated because you partly *create* the landscape you will travel through) but other aspects fall into place rather nicely.

BEING AN EXPLORER

The key to being an explorer is having an attitude that prevents you from getting stuck. You must be determined, creative and open to the subtle hints that indicate your progress. You have to be able to think and react quickly. You should also not be overly result-focussed, but ready to learn your way towards a solution. The rest follows from this basic attitude.

Having this attitude, you use the available knowledge about the exploration area (maps), you are familiar with different exploration strategies and you know when to use them. You will also have a collection of frames that has been gathered from prior experience (the usual structure of a mountain range), and practical expertise for the most concrete problems (How to Wrestle an Alligator). To begin to explore you should just set out in the general direction where you expect the solution to be. But when you come up against some barrier, and you can't go on, what should you do? There are many options – you can try to go over the obstacle, around it, or to hack your way through it. You can also try to ignore the problem, or just whine. You can even deny that there is a problem. However, it is probably more productive to sit back and think about it (has this happened before?) or to get more information (study the maps). If the worst happens, you must just turn back and report what you have learned.

If we translate this metaphor back to design, a recent court case can serve as an example. The client sued a design firm because it had developed a product that did not work, but had nonetheless made it onto the market. What happened in the project was that the initial product concept wasn't very strong. In every stage, new problems surfaced and were patched with extra parts. As a result, the design had become more and more complicated. Apparently the design firm had passed the point where they felt they could elegantly backtrack and start over. So they went on with the increasingly horrid design, never daring to admit failure. The derailed design project should have been stopped by the client, but they trusted the design firm to provide the technical expertise.

This project violates almost every rule of a good exploration. It was doomed from the start.

NO END

The exploratory nature of design is the reason this book tries to approach questions of design in many different ways – in design, there is not one general answer to anything. There are many possible views of design, and many routes out of a problematic design situation – a designer had better be flexible in using them.

A good exploration ends, of course, when you have found what you were looking for. And if you have been conscious of your decisions and their repercussions, you will have learned a lot from the exploration itself. Next time it will be easier to arrive at a solution. Having come to the result, you will probably also get a serious bout of post-project depression, because finding the route towards the solution is always the best part. You'll want to set out again.

Each design project is a new world to explore. And although each design project is unique, there are patterns to the design landscape, which you begin to be aware of as you explore further. Experience will deepen your understanding of your work, and help to find ever more clever approaches.

The pieces in this book are based on design research, my personal experience, and those of the designers I know. I hope they help designers to reflect upon their practice. But there are limits to what a book can do: you really only learn and master things that you can relate to your own experience – the core design experiences that you feel and live through cannot be borrowed from others.

Nothing beats designing.

REFERENCES
& INDEX

REFERENCES

In this book I pass on many lessons from my mentors and colleagues: the designers, teachers and scientists who inspired me in my reflections, and who will hopefully inspire the reader as well. An overview of their works can be found here, and all are highly recommended.

PART 1: INSIDE DESIGN

Design as ...

Design as Applied Creativity

... a report on this study can be found in: Lawson BR (1997) Cognitive Strategies in Architectural Design, in: Cross NG (1984) *Developments in Design Methodology* Wiley, Chichester (this book is *the* overview of the first 20 years of design research)

Design as Problem Solving

... there are many good textbooks that teach the models and methods of design: Cross NG (1994) *Engineering Design Methods* (2nd Ed) Wiley, Chichester

Roozenburg NFM (1995) Eekels J, *Product Design: Fundamentals and Methods* Wiley, Chichester

Ullman DG (1992) *The Mechanical Design Process* McGraw-Hill, NY

Ulrich KT (1995) Eppinger S D *Product Design and Development* McGraw-Hill, NY

VDI (1987) *VDI 2221: Systematic Approach to the Design of Technical Systems and Products* Beuth Verlag, Berlin

Design as Learning

... the quote is from: Alexander C (1971) The state of the art in design methods, in: Cross NG (1984) *Developments in Design Methodology* Wiley, Chichester

... design as learning was introduced in: Schön DA (1982) *The Reflective Practitioner* Basic Books, NY

Design as a Social Process

... the seminal book on the social side of design is: Bucciarelli LL (1994) *Designing Engineers* MIT Press, Boston

Design Problems

Wicked problems / Problem and Solution as Siamese Twins

... the properties of design problems are discussed extensively in: Lawson BR (2006) *How designers think: the design process demystified*

(4th ed) Architectural Press, London

Design Solutions

What Designers Make

... a well-written journalistic description of a development project in the automobile industry: Walton M (1997) *Car* WW. Norton & company, NY

Kinds of Designing

Knowledge Structure

... there are many books about the teaching methods of the Bauhaus, like: Poling CV (1986) *Kandinsky's teaching at the Bauhaus - colour theory and analytical drawing* Rizzolli, NY

Traditions and Rituals

... about the ethnographic method for investigating designers' behaviour: Bucciarelli LL (1994) *Designing Engineers* MIT Press, Boston

Roles of Designers

... on the efficient running of a product development operation: Clark KB and Fuijmoto T (1991) *Product Development Performance* Harvard Business School Press, Boston MA

... the book about the design of a new computer: Kidder T (1981) *The Soul of a New Machine* Penguin Books, NY

Success

Hart S (1996) The Methodological Issues in the Theoretical Development and Validity of S/F Measurement, in: Thoelke J, Loosschilder G, Smulders F, *Hidden versus Open Rules in Product Development*, TU Delft, Faculty of Industrial Design Engineering

Elements of Design

The Resolution of Conflicts

...for more depth in this subject and further references see: Dorst CH (2006) Design Problems and Design Paradoxes, *Design Issues* Vol 22, No 3, pp 4-17

... the quote is from: Whitbeck C (1998) *Ethics in Engineering Practice and Research* Cambridge University Press, UK

Moulding the Design Situation

... this example is taken from: Hatchuel A (2002) Towards design theory and expandable rationality: the unfinished program of Herbert Simon *Journal of Management and Governance* Vol 5, No 3-4, pp 260-273

Why Designers Don't Document their Projects

... the quote is from: Wittgenstein L (1953) *Philosophical investigations* Basil Blackwell, Oxford

How To...?

Information

... all quotes of designers in these and other chapters are (unless stated otherwise) taken from the great paper on the nature and teaching of design: Cross NG (1990) The Nature and Nurture of the Design Ability, *Design Studies* Vol 11, No 3

Overviews

... the idea of using design sessions in this way is from: Reymen IMMJ (2001*) Improving Design Processes through Structured Reflection* Thesis TU Eindhoven

Designing a Context

... the design of a context is championed by: Hekkert PPM (2001) van Dijk MB, Designing from Context: Foundations and Applications of the ViP Approach, in: Lloyd P, Christiaans HCCM (eds) *Designing in Context* Delft University Press, Delft

Rules of Thumb

... this research was done by Danielle Hendriks – and reported in papers like: Hendriks DJHC, Dorst CH (2001) Design project management in practice –the email diary study, in: Culey S et al. (eds) *ICED 01*, Professional Engineering Publishing, London

Primary Generators

... the quote is from: Rowe PG (1987) *Design thinking* MIT Press, Cambridge MA

PART 2: ABOUT DESIGN

Thinking about Design

Design Science: The Pleasure of Abstraction

... see the textbooks that are listed under Design as Problem Solving

Screenwriting

Field S (1984) *Screenwriter's Workbook* Dell Publishing, NY

The Experience of Designing

Inside Design

… the notion of 'Flow' was presented in: Csikszentmihalyi M (1990) *Flow* Harper Collins

Laying Down a Path in Walking

…a treatise on human problem solving that is heavily influenced by Eastern (Zen) philosophy: Varela FJ (1991), Thompson E Rosch E *The embodied mind* MIT Press, Cambridge MA

Platypus

… the platypus-metaphor is an adaptation from: Pirsig RM (1991) *Lila* Bantam, NY

Thrownness

…the notion of 'thrownness' was introduced into design literature in: Winograd T (1986) Flores F *Understanding computers and cognition* Ablex, Norwood NJ

Mr. Heidegger

…the phenomenological theory of Heidegger is applied to human problem solving in: Dreyfus HL (1992) *What Computers still can't do* MIT Press, Cambridge MA

Education

Reflection

…the first book that stressed the role of reflection in design was: Schön DA (1983) *The Reflective Practitioner* Basic Books, NY

…its sequel details a programme of reflective education: Schön DA (1987) *Educating the Reflective Practitioner* Jossey-Bass Publishers, SF

The Guy from Practice

Goldschmidt (2003) Expert knowledge or creative spark? Predicaments in design education, in: Cross NG, Edmonds E *Expertise in Design, Design Thinking Research Symposium 6*, Creativity & Cognition Studios Press, Sydney

Levels of Excellence

McCloud S (1994) *Understanding comics* Harper Perennial, NY

Snowballing

… the quote is from the Dutch writer Bomans: Bomans G (1977) *Aforismen* Elsevier, Amsterdam

The Evolution of a Designer

Dreyfus HL (2002) Intelligence without representation – Merleau-Ponty's critique of mental representation, *Phenomenology and the Cognitive Sciences*, Vol 1, pp 367-383

Dreyfus HL (2002) *What Computers Still Can't Do* MIT Press, Cambridge MA

... two books on design expertise: Lawson B, Dorst CH (2007) *Becoming a Designer*, Architectural Press London (in print)

Cross NG (2006) *Designerly Ways of Knowing*, Springer Verlag, London

PART 3: BEING A DESIGNER

On Designers

The Design Ability

...the list of abilities is taken from the comprehensive paper on the nature and teaching of design: Cross NG (1990) The Nature and Nurture of the Design Ability, *Design Studies* Vol 11, No 3

Psychology of Design

...the multiple intelligences were introduced in: Gardner H (1983) *Frames of Mind: the Theory of Multiple Intelligences* Heinemann, London

Gardner H (1993) *Creating Minds* Basic Books, NY

Creative Minds

Darwin's Eureka that Never Was

... the story about Darwin is from: Gould SJ (1982) Darwin's Middle Road, in: *The Panda's Thumb* Norton, NY

Brainstorming

... a good book on the extensive creative problem solving method is: Isaksen S G (1994) Dorval K B & Treffinger D J *Creative approaches to problem solving* Kendall & Hunt, Dubuque, IA

Head Heart Hand

'The Quality Without a Name'

... the term Quality Without a Name (from the Tao Te Ching) was first applied to design in: Alexander C (1979) *The Timeless Way of Building* Oxford University Press, NY

Motorcycle Maintenance

Pirsig RM (1974) *Zen and the art of motorcycle maintenance* Bantam, NY

Thinking Tools for Designers

Functions

... the use of functions and the methods associated with them is treated in the textbooks listed under 'The Pleasure of Abstraction'.

Strategies

... an extensive report on this research project can be found in: Dorst CH (1997) *Describing Design* Thesis TU Delft

Design Teams

Shared Understanding

... the specialist treatise on the behaviour of design teams: Valkenburg AC (2000) *The Reflective Practice in Product Design Teams* Thesis TU Delft

Divergent Pairs

... the idea of hiring in divergent pairs comes from a book that takes a refreshing look at the creation and management of a design firm: Hirshberg J (1999) *The Creative Priority* Harper Business, NY

The Winning Team

The 'explosion' metaphor was coined by Dick Powell, of the UK design firm Seymour and Powell, in a BBC TV interview in the series 'Designs on your ...'.

PART 4: AROUND DESIGN

Designing in Context

Natural Enemies

A very clear investigation of these interface-issues can be found in: Smulders FEHM (2006) *Get Synchronized! Bridging the Gap Between Design & Volume Production* Thesis TU Delft

ISO 9000 and the Holy Process

... the standards referred to are ISO 9000-9004, notably *ISO 9001*.

Managing Design

The Wall of Secrecy

... the Boston firm *Product Genesis* takes this approach to its clients.

Design morality

Risks and Disasters

... stories of failure and lessons for success can be found in: Petrosky H (1985) *To Engineer is Human: The Role of Failure in Successful Design* St Martin's Press, NY

... the Citicorp story was told in: Whitbeck C (1998) *Ethics in Engineering Practice and Research* Cambridge University Press, UK

I Just Work Here

... the list of classic excuses comes from: Zandvoort H (2001) Bonnet JABAF *Ethiek en STM* TU Delft

PART 5: DESIGN IN THE REAL WORLD

Design as a Way of Thinking

Applying Design Thinking

... the example is taken from the chapter Why The Sea Is Blue, in: Colinvaux PA (1980) *Why Big Fierce Animals Are Rare* Penguin Books

Medieval Thinking

... this is based on: Foucault M (1970) *The Order Of Things* Random House

Design and society

Design versus the Real World

Papanek V (1974) *Design for the Real World* Paladin, St Albans

Past

The Evolution of Things

... the example is taken from: Bijker WE (1995) *Of Bicycles, Bakelites, Bulbs - Toward a Theory of Sociotechnical Change* MIT Press, Cambridge MA

...thedisastrousreactionstothefuturearefrom:LawsonBR(2006)*Howdesignersthink:thedesignprocessdemystified* (4th ed) Architectural Press, London

Design Debates

Does Form Follow Function?

... this argument is loosely based on: Good JV, Good P (2001) Is Functionalism Functional? in: Holland DK (ed), *Design Issues* Alworth, NY

The Three Qualities

Royakkers LMM, Dorst CH (2006) The Ethical Cycle and Judgment in Design, in DRS, *Proceedings of the Wonderground conference*, Lisbon

Everlasting Debates and their Resolution

... the wry quote is from: Warhol A (1975) *THE Philosophy of Andy Warhol* Harcourt Brace & Co, San Diego

Future

Technophilia and Technophobia

A clear case of Technophilia: Mau B (2004) *Massive Change*, Phaidon Press London

Design for Debate

See *www.dunneandraby.co.uk* for an impressive overview of projects & writings. Very much recommended!

The Designer and the Pyramid

For an interesting insight into the relationship between service design and the design of physical objects: Meijkamp RG (2000) *Changing Consumer Behaviour through Eco-efficient Services* Thesis TU Delft

Design Connects

... for practice-based research methods developed and used by designers, see the IDEO Method Cards (www.ideo.com) and the book: Laurel B (ed.) (2003) *Design Research – Methods and Perspectives* MIT Press, Cambridge MA

... everything you always wanted to know about Collaborative Design can be found in *CoDesign – International Journal of CoCreation in Design and the Arts* Taylor & Francis, London

Solving the Unsolvable Problem/ Designing Our Way to the Future

... groundbreaking projects in which design is used to create solutions for social problems are initiated and executed by YD+I, see *www.YDI.nl*.

PART 6: SUMMING UP

A Metaphor for Design

Metaphors we Live By

... the notion of metaphors as active structuring element in our lives can be found in: Lakoff G Johnson M (1980) *Metaphors We Live By* The University of Chicago Press, Chicago IL

INDEX

BIOGRAPHY

Kees Dorst was trained as an Industrial Design Engineer at Delft University of Technology, and studied some philosophy at the Erasmus University Rotterdam. Since obtaining his degree in 1989 he has worked as a product designer for various design firms, participating in about fifty projects. At the same time he worked as a researcher in Design Studies at the TU Delft. In his thesis 'Describing Design – A Comparison of Paradigms' (1997, Cum Laude) he compared two fundamentally different ways of describing design processes: Rational Problem Solving and Reflective Practice. He has lectured at universities and design schools throughout the world, and has been on the editorial board of the main Dutch Design magazine Items.

Currently, Kees Dorst is Professor of Design at the faculty of Design, Architecture and Building of the University of Technology, Sydney (Australia) and Senior Design Researcher at the Department of Industrial Design at Eindhoven University of Technology (The Netherlands). He also teaches design methods at the Design Academy Eindhoven and at various management institutes in The Netherlands, and works as a consultant in the fields of product design and product development. He is advisor to Young Designers and Industry and the Amsterdam Creativity Exchange, and a regular contributor to the magazine of the Dutch Designers Association BNO. He has published numerous articles and three books. For more information and downloads: www.keesdorst.nl.

COLOPHON

Concept/Author: Kees Dorst
English editing: Phyllis Crabill
Design: Studio Ron van Roon, Amsterdam

BIS Publishers
Herengracht 370-372
1016 CH Amsterdam
P.O. Box 323
1000 AH Amsterdam
The Netherlands
T +31 20 524 75 60
F +31 20 524 75 57
bis@bispublishers.nl
www.bispublishers.nl

ISBN 90-6369-149-1
ISBN 978-90-6369-149-3

© 2003/2006 BIS Publishers, Amsterdam